Troll
Louse
Kookies

WILLIAM M. SCHMALFELDT, SR.

DEDICATION

Through the 367 Criminal Charges, through the three peace orders, through
the Copyright Infringement Suit, the constant insults and threats and
portents of doom from my gaggle of trolls, one person continues to love
me and stand by me and yell at me when I need yelling at. Thank you, Gail.
I love you with all my heart..

CONTENTS

ACKNOWLEDGMENTS

In the summer of 2013, I received some graphic death threats via e-mail. This vile person promised to tie me to my bed, gut my dogs and rape my wife while I watched. I called the Howard County, Maryland, Police and showed them the e-mail. Their advice? "Get off the Internet and they'll leave you alone. But call us if you get killed," or words to that effect. Acknowledgements in books are usually intended to be positive. However I would be remiss if I failed to tell the reader how many times I have called on the law enforcement establishment of this county, a neighboring county, this state, this nation's government, to protect this disabled veteran, this retired person with Stage IV Parkinson's disease, only to be told, in effect, don't dress so sexy if ya don't wanna get raped.

To local, state and federal law enforcement. Wake the hell up. This is the 21st Century. Crimes are being committed and you are apparently unable to protect the people you are charged with protecting.

1 HEY! THESE KOOKIES HAVE NUTS!

The sound cut through my nightly thanatopsis, the period most call sleep but I think of as "rehearsal for being dead."

"Arroooghaaaroo."

That's as close as I can come to spelling it. It wasn't a loud "arroooghaaaroo." That would have been impolite. It was a soft, almost whispered "arroooghaaaroo", reminiscent of a child poking its sleeping father on his closed eyelid, whispering, "Daddy? Are you awake? Daddy?"

Only this was not a child at the side of my bed. It was an 8-year old Chinook. Something akin to a German Shepherd, but not nearly as regal. I opened my eyes and turned to see the two black eyes, the pointy ears standing straight up, a cheerful smile on her face, and a happy tail wagging back and forth.

"What the Hell do you want," I asked as I scratched her head. She started licking my hand.

"Is she bothering you," my wife asked from the other bed in the room.

"Nah, she's just kissing me up a little," I said.

Gail, my wife of nearly 25-years and my primary

caretaker since my 15-years with Parkinson's disease have left me fairly unable to do stuff, sat up on the edge of the bed and looked down the hallway toward the living room.

"I don't know what she wants," Gail said. "She's already crapped on the living room rug."

"Maybe she just wants to brag about it," I offered.

Gail got up, a happy, tail-wagging Chinook and a sleepy, grumpy 10-year old border collie named Raven followed her from the bedroom.

I was awake and there really wasn't much of a chance of drifting off to sleep soon. So I grabbed the iPad next to my bed to see if there were any new death threats in the email, or anything interesting like that.

There was a note from my son, a third-generation nerd living in Florida.

"Not 100% your case, but thought this article was a good read about Internet dick heads."

Peter certainly inherited his father's way with words.

I clicked the link and there was a story written by a pseudonymous blogger, who I will not name in order to not invite more harassment than she's already received.

Her story wasn't 100% my case, so Peter was correct in that regard. But it was pretty damn close. Maybe 97%.

In her opening paragraph, she gives blanket permission to redistribute the work. So, here it is. It's called **"Trouble at the Koolaid Point."**

October 7, 2014

[Note: I didn't want to have to write this. But here it is. I'm not linking it to the blog, and it won't likely stay up long, but you are welcome to contact me here if you want to put it somewhere else before I take it down. It is long and rambling and unedited and one of the few

things I've written that I wrote mostly for myself. It is all I ever hope to have to say about it. Also? Content warning.]

This month is the 10-year anniversary of my first online threat. I thought it was a one-off, then. Just one angry guy. And it wasn't really *THAT* bad. But looking back, it was the canary in the coal mine... the first hint that if I kept on this path, it would not end well. And what was that path? We'll get to that in a minute.

Later I learned that the first threat had nothing to do with what I actually *made* or *said* in my books, blog posts, articles, and conference presentations. The *real* problem — as my first harasser described — was that *others were beginning to pay attention* to me. He wrote as if mere exposure to my work was harming his world.

But here's the key: it turned out he wasn't outraged about my work. His rage was because, in his mind, my work didn't *deserve* the *attention*. Spoiler alert: "deserve" and "attention" are at the heart.

A year later, I wrote a light-hearted article about "haters" (the quotes matter) and something I called The Koolaid Point. It wasn't about harassment, abuse, or threats against *people* but about the kind of brand "trolls" you find in, say, Apple discussion forums. My wildly non-scientific theory was this: the most vocal trolling and "hate" for a brand kicks in HARD once a critical mass of brand fans/users are thought to have "drunk the Koolaid". In other words, the hate wasn't so much about the product/brand but that *other people were falling for it.*

I was delighted, a few weeks' later, to see my little "Koolaid Point" in Wired's Jargon Watch column.

The me of 2005 had no idea what was coming.

Less than two years later, I'd learn that my festive take on harmless *brand* trolling also applied to *people.* And it wasn't festive. Or harmless. Especially for women.

I now believe the most dangerous time for a woman with online visibility is the point at which others are seen to be listening, "following", "liking", "favoriting", retweeting. In other words, the point at which her readers have (in the troll's mind) "drunk the Koolaid". Apparently, that just can't be allowed.

From the hater's POV, you (the Koolaid *server*) do not "deserve" that attention. You are "stealing" an audience. From their angry, frustrated point of view, the idea that others listen to you is insanity. From their emotion-fueled view you don't have readers you have cult followers. That just can't be allowed.

You must be stopped. And if they cannot stop you, they can at least ruin your quality of life. A standard goal, in troll culture, I soon learned, is to cause "personal ruin". They aren't all *trolls*, though. Some of those who seek to stop and/or ruin you are misguided/misinformed but well-intended. They actually believe in a cause, and they believe you (or rather the Koolaid you're serving) threatens that cause.

But the Koolaid-Point-driven attacks are usually started by (speculating, educated guess here, not an actual psychologist, etc) sociopaths. They're doing it out of pure malice, "for the lulz." And those doing it for the lulz are masters at manipulating public perception. Master trolls can build an online army out of the well-intended, by appealing to The Cause (more on that later). The very best/worst trolls can even make the non-sociopaths believe "for the lulz" is itself a noble cause.

But I actually got off easy, then. Most of the master trolls weren't active on Twitter in 2007. Today, they, along with their friends, fans, followers, and a zoo of anonymous sock puppet accounts *are*. The time from troll-has-an-idea to troll-mobilizes-brutal-assault has shrunk from weeks to minutes. Twitter, for all its good, is a hate amplifier. Twitter boosts signal power with head-snapping speed and strength. Today, Twitter (and this isn't a complaint about Twitter, it's about what Twitter enables) is the troll's best weapon for attacking you. And by "you", I mean "you the server of Koolaid." You who must be stopped.

It begins with simple threats. You know, rape, dismemberment, the usual. It's a good place to start, those threats, because you might simply vanish once those threats include your family. Mission accomplished. But today, many women online — you women who are far braver than I am — you stick around. And now, since you stuck around through the first wave of threats, you are now a much BIGGER problem. Because the Worst Possible Thing has happened: as a result of those attacks, you are NOW serving *Victim*-Flavored Koolaid.

And *Victim*-Flavored Koolaid is the most dangerous substance on earth, apparently. And that just can't be allowed.

There is only one reliably useful weapon for the trolls to stop the danger you pose and/or to get max lulz: *discredit you.* The disinformation follows a pattern so predictable today it's almost dull: first, you obviously "fucked" your way into whatever role enabled your undeserved visibility. I mean..*duh*. A woman. In tech. Not that there aren't a few deserving women and why can't you be more like THEM but no, you are NOT one of them.

You are, they claim, CLEARLY "a whore". But not the sex-worker kind, no, you are the Bad Kind of Whore. Actually TWO kinds: an Attention/Fame Whore and an Actual Have Sex In Exchange For Jobs, Good Reviews, Book Deals Whore. I mean, could there be ANY other explanation for your visibility? But the sex-not-merit meme is just their warm-up, the lowest-hanging-fruit in a discredit/disinfo campaign.

Because what the haters MOST want the world to know is this: what you're serving your audience? It's

NOT EVEN ACTUAL KOOLAID. "Snake oil", the trolls insist. You're a "proven liar". Or, as I was referred to yet again just yesterday by *my* favorite troll/hater/harasser: "a charlatan". And there is "evidence". There is always "evidence". (there isn't, of course, but let's not let that get in the way.)

And the trolls aren't stupid. The most damaging troll/haters are some of the most powerful people (though they self-describe as outcasts). Typically, the hacker trolls are technically-talented, super smart white men. They're not just hackers. They are *social engineers.* They understand behavioral psych. They know their Kahneman. They "get" memes. They exploit a vulnerability in the brains of your current and potential listeners.

How? By unleashing a mind virus guaranteed to push emotional buttons for your real, NOT-troll audience. In my specific case, it was my alleged threat to a free and open internet. "She issued DMCA takedowns for sites that criticized her." Yes, that one even made it's way into a GQ magazine article not long ago, when the writer Sanjiv Bhattacharya interviewed weev and asked about — get this — the "ethics" of doxxing me. Weev's explanation was just one more leveling up in my discredit/disinfo program: DMCA takedowns. I had, apparently, issued DMCA takedowns.

If you are in the tech world, issuing a DMCA takedown is worse than kicking puppies off a pier. But what I did? It was (according to the meme) much much worse. *I* did it (apparently) to *stifle criticism.* If a DMCA takedown is kicking puppies, doing it to "stifle criticism" is like single-handedly causing the extinction of puppies, kittens, and the constitution. Behold my awesome and terrible power. Go me.

But here's the thing. I never did that. I never did anything even a teeny tiny nano bit like that. But sure enough, even on my last day on Twitter, there it was again: Kathy did DMCA's. And it wasn't even a troll saying it, *it was another woman in tech* who believed the meme because she believed weev. Because in twisted troll logic, it makes sense. She *must* have done something *pretty awful* to deserve what, according to weev, "she had coming."

After the GQ story came out, the one where weev "justified" the harassment of me by introducing the DMCA fiction, I asked him about it on Twitter. "Where, seriously, where exactly did I ever issue a DMCA?" His answer? Oh, right, he didn't have an answer. Because it didn't happen. But see? he doesn't have to. He's already launched the Kathy-does-DMCA-takedowns meme. Evidence not required. For that matter, common sense not required.

(For the record, far as most people have been able to determine, most of what happened to me long ago was triggered by a blog comment I made that said "I'm not moderating my blog comments, but I support those who do and here's why." That's right, Blog. Comment. Moderation. Just a tiny hop, really, from that to full-blown DMCA takedowns. Easy mistake.)

For me, the hot button to rally the army (including the Good People) against me was my (totally fictional) legal threat to freedom. But there are *so* many other hot buttons to use against women in tech. So. Many.

A particularly robust troll-crafted hot button meme today is that *some women are out to destroy video games* (shoutout to #gamergaters). Another is that they are taking jobs from men. Men who are, I mean obviously, more deserving. "If women/minorities/any oppressed group are given special treatment, that's not equality," they argue "I guess you don't believe in equality, feminists." Quickly followed by, "wait, did I say 'oppressed group'? There's no such thing as an oppressed group I just meant Professional Victims Who Pretend To Be Oppressed And Serve Social Justice Warrior Koolaid."

Life for women in tech, today, is often better the less visible they are. Less visible means fewer perceived Koolaid drinkers.

"Oy!" I thought. I am not a woman in tech. In fact, I am neither a woman nor in tech. (Nor am I Jewish, despite the Judaic expression of angst.) But change a few facts, a name here, a circumstance there, and this person was writing about my last two years!.

For I also am a deranged sociopath cyberstalker who must be stopped. It has been written in blogs! Therefore, it must be true!

According to a recent addition to the Official Doctrine, it would seem that my wife (who was currently removing Shiloh's leavings from the living room) has to bear some of the blame for the evil I bring to the world with my evil evilness and villainy.

This is one of 293 comments currently posted on a blog that seems to be devoted to my murder, suicide, or whatever else will get me started on my eventual dirt nap, sooner rather than later. It was written by someone with the ironic name of "Grace." She discusses a "secret site" created by the blog owner where the people who wish this dire fate upon me can gather and plot and plan in password-protected secrecy, away from my prying eyes.

October 6, 2014 at 3:44 pm

Typical Bill… entirely avoids addressing being called out on his latest FAIL. It just knots his knickers that things may be being said about him that he cannot read. And, why would anyone need to be worried about SECURITY on that site? Maybe The Elkridge Horror would like to provide some clarity. Is he threatening the integrity of that site? I guess if anything were to happen to that site — hacking, what not — someone would know who to focus their attention on now, wouldn't they?

And, it appears the Deranged Cyberstalker and Adjudicated Harasser Bill Schmalfeldt believes his "I'd be careful" threat means something to me. Newsflash: It doesn't.

I most certainly consider any "woman" who would marry such a heinous and evil monster to be a HAG.

Any "woman" who FOR YEARS ignores/allows/encourages /participates in her husband-

the-sociopath's harassment, stalking, and threats against men, women, and CHILDREN is a HAG.

A HUGE, UGLY, NASTY HAG.

And, if by chance — mind you... a very, very, very small chance — the HAG is completely and utterly oblivious to this psychopath's:

Online and Real Life Harassment of others

Online and Real Life Stalking of others

Threats to have children taken away from a mother

Wicked abuse of a grieving mother over her stillborn daughter

Numerous court dates

Peace Orders

Restraining Orders

Rape Fantasy

Pornographic Photoshops

Copyright Infringement

Hate Books

Filing of False Reports

Being canned from numerous sites due to lies, libel, and

anti-social behavior

Friendship with a domestic terrorist who has a sick fondness for minor girls

Blogs that post images of children and personal, private information

Radio shows discussing children in the most vile of ways

Stalking/harassment of a rape victim

Posting address/pic of home belonging to someone who just received a rape threat

HOURS-UPON-HOURS EVERYDAY AT HIS COMPUTER!

Etc. Etc. Etc. Etc. Etc.

... then is she not only a HAG — she is the most clueless and most stupid HAG to have ever lived.

Well. THAT'S unfair. My wife used to have a weight problem, but since surviving cancer, she's gone from nearly 300 lbs. to a svelte 140. But that is a "truth" and it doesn't fit in with the official Doctrine or "Canon" of this particular religion.

I have never harassed anyone online, although one man lied to a judge about the actual fact that I used the @reply function on Twitter to refer to him. He convinced the judge that this constituted "direct contact" and he was in fear for his life and limb from this man who can no longer walk unassisted and can barely raise his arms over his head.

How can I "stalk" anyone when I haven't driven a car since 2009 and would require Gail's assistance to drive me to where this "stalking" would take place?

I've never threatened to take children away from a mother. I did once tell a drunken sleaze in Wisconsin that if the media found out she was ignoring her children to booze it up and get funky with a guy who wasn't her hubby, Child Welfare might want to have a look at her situation.

WHAT "wicked abuse of a grieving mother over her stillborn daughter?" I did ask a right wing columnist why he told three different versions of the unfortunate event, so that must be what the "wicked abuse" consisted of.

Numerous court dates? That's MY fault, that a vexatious, vindictive old loser wants to take his anger out on me for the failure of his own life?

Restraining Orders? We covered that in the paragraph where I told you how the man lied to a judge.

"Rape Fantasy"? Jesus! Talk about Koolaid drinkers. We'll discuss this alleged "rape fantasies" in an upcoming chapter.

"Pornographic Photoshops?" Not one. Ever. Crude? Yeah. But pornographic? Not even close.

"Copyright Infringement?" That has been settled. The plaintiff wanted $620,000 and walked away with $0.

"Hate Books?" Well, I guess any book I write would be a "hate book" to Grace and her ilk (and what an ilk it is!) since I tend to disagree and disprove the official Doctrine and Canon.

"Filing of False Reports"? When? Where? To Whom? Or does Grace have judicial power to declare legitimate reports "true" or "false"?

"Being canned from numerous sites due to lies (never),

libel (no ma'am) and anti-social behavior?" If you mean disagreeing with Daily Kos commenters is "anti-social," I suppose she has me there. That's one site. The other is the conservative rag "Examiner.com" which hired me back.

"Friendship with a domestic terrorist who has a sick fondness for minor girls?" Who are we talking about? I don't know anyone who has been convicted of "domestic terrorism" or "pedophilia." Of course, Grace has the power over truth and falsehood, so what can I say?

"Blogs that post pictures of children and personal, private information?" I've never posted a picture of a child that wasn't already posted online. And personal and private in this case means information easily accessible online to anyone who wants it.

"Stalking/harassment of a rape victim?" I don't even know who Grace is talking about here. I wonder if she does.

"Posting address/pic of home belonging to someone who had just received a rape threat?" Except she never received a rape threat, and her hubby was sending their address via e-mail to anyone who asked for it, which is how I got it.

"HOURS-UPON-HOURS EVERY DAY AT HIS COMPUTER!" What am I supposed to do? Go jogging? I'm retired. I have a disabling, degenerative neurological disorder. I write. I run an online radio station. And I bet you a donut that Grace spends far more time at HER spit-flecked computer than I do at mine. (Yes, I do have to occasionally have to clean up spit flecks.)

This is why I am known as "The Elkridge Horror." It's OK if they post MY home address. It's OK if they post my private information. It's OK if they send me death threats and suggest that I kill myself or they'll do it for me. All that is perfectly fine because THEY are GOOD and

RIGHTEOUS and I am the EVIL ONE!

I can almost hear her cackling like a witch as she wrote that…

2 THE TROLLS PACK THEIR OWN LUNCH

Much has been written as of late about the best way to handle and deal with Internet trolls who have become fixated on you.

An article by Suzanne Moore in the Oct. 7, 2014 edition of The Guardian discusses whether or not "free speech" guarantees the right to anonymous trolling.

This is a hot topic across the pond these days, as someone who was identified as a person trolling the family of a missing girl was, herself, found dead.

Ms. Moore writes:

Those who sent abusive messages about this case are seen by some to be warriors against the lies and evils of the mainstream media. Trolling, they say, is just another word for challenging.

Though social media is now so deeply embedded, we still don't seem to have any shared social definitions of what trolling is. It continues to be seen as somehow trivial, just silly insulting nonsense that should be ignored.

But you can only regard it this way if you have never experienced it. Trolling can be an orchestrated and concerted campaign to intimidate others into silence.

Multiple threats of death, rape and mutilation, as well as the publication of addresses (as much as Twitter wants to refuse this role, platforms act as publishers) is the modus operandi that brought a lot of misogyny to the surface. Trolling can also be obsessive and highly personalised – a form of stalking.

Calls for action are often tokenistic. Twitter could never employ enough moderators to look at every tweet.

Let me take it a step further than that, Ms. Moore.

Twitter does not CARE! It is not in their BUSINESS MODEL to care about trolling. Twitter understands that if all the trolls are banned, Twitter will cease to exist. Twitter NEED trolls to make money. I can't tell you how many times I have complained to Twitter, filled out form after form, identified the offending tweet, only to experience their quick and instant justice with MY account being suspended.

They say, "Don't feed the trolls."

The trolls pack their own lunch.

They say, "Just ignore them and they'll go away."

The truth is, they will just find new and more obnoxious ways to troll you. They will send you e-mails. They will post filthy comments on your blogs. They will write false reviews for products you are trying to sell on Amazon. And if that doesn't work, they will try to kill you.

Or get you to kill yourself.

The trolling gets more and more obnoxious the more you ignore them.

My mom died of congestive heart failure on March 8, 2013. Here is a picture of her taken two months before.

Muz was enjoying a hunk of a nice cheesecake I sent for her and my sister in Milwaukee to share. Here's what one Internet Troll did with that picture.

Howard D. Earl

@embryriddlealum

I'm 100% positive. No doubt, whatsoever that I am NOT Jerry Fletcher or Robin Causey. Pointer and Laugher at Inspector Jiggles Enterprises.

Delightful, yes? Here's another one. From 1976 when I was on leave from the Navy, visiting my Mom and Dad.

All that lovely hair. The trolls liked this picture, too!

TWEETS
159

Shaky McSpittle
@ParkinsonsHumor

Get it? Shaky? Because I have Parkinson's disease. Making fun of my disease is part and parcel for this crew.

But I don't want you to think that it was just my dead mother the Trolls found amusing. They also enjoyed pictures of my father, who died of pancreatic cancer in 1983.

Howard D. Earl @embryriddlealum · May 3
@guntotingteabag @palatinepundit @brainsrfood I found a pic of his dad, too.

↩ Reply   ⇄ Retweet   ★ Favorite

Oh, these jolly, jolly trolls.

And my wife. No reason to leave her out of the fun, right "Grace"?

Let's take a picture from one of my websites from when she was battling (and beating) throat cancer and, because she recently tripped and fell, turn it into an "abusive husband" meme!

disagreement?--> @BlitzParkinsons <-- @CoulsonJason @mayberryville

       2   View conversation

Howard D. Earl @embryriddlealum · Sep 30

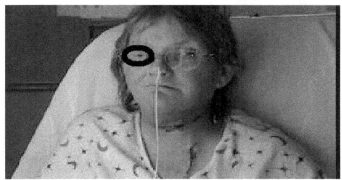

Hi Larious!

TWEETS

26

Gayle Smallfield

@captivenurse

Trapped by one bad decision

But you see, if you just walk away and ignore them, they will leave you alone. Right?

Meh. Not so much. This trolling goes back to 2012 when I was doing some writing about a group of right wing Wisconsin knuckleheads trying to interfere with the petition gathering in the recall of Gov. Walker.

Operation Burn Notice
This hour is brought to you by the CURE FOR PARKINSON'S DISEASE.

Like · Comment · Share · Sunday at 2:54pm ·

5 people like this.

Howard D. Earl @embryriddlealum · Nov 13
@guntotingteabag The CURE

View more photos and videos

Yes, my having Stage IV Parkinson's disease has been quite the source of amusement for this bunch.

But somehow, so far anyway, I have refused their demands that I die at my own hand.

Howard D. Earl
@embryriddlealum

⚙ +⚑ Follow

@DeepBrainRadio @antvq16 @guntotingteabag The cure, Shaky. THE CURE!

↩ Reply ⇄ Retweet ★ Favorite ••• More

8:07 AM - 2 Dec 2013

The other day, I received what I perceive to be a statement of impatience for my forcing these idiots to have to wait for me to die.

It was coupled with the announcement that this particular troll would continue to act as he had been acting, including the potential creation of a website that exists only to defame my deceased family members.

Howard D. Earl (@embryriddlealum)   **October 4, 2014 at 10:40 am**

👍 4 👎 5 ⊘ Rate This

You poor dumb bastard (literally), Shakey. You are too dumb and far too obtuse to ever realize that you have never posted a pic that has anything to do with me. You have no idea who I am. You have never even been close.

You will know who I am on your death bed. I will make sure of it. And hopefully it will be soon.

Reply

 Howard D. Earl (@embryriddlealum)   **October 4, 2014 at 10:45 am**

👍 3 👎 6 ⊘ Rate This

I will take it upon myself now, to post the most vile photos, of every one of Bill Schmalfeldt's family members.

Did your mom ever blow a donkey?

Did your dad service Muslim prisoners?

Does Gail work Balmer street corners?

Photographic proof coming soon.Because I know who THEY are.

Be looking for my new wordpress site.

But by all means, keep doing what you're doing.

Reply

24

It almost makes me feel bad for staying alive since this dipshit is so looking forward to my being dead.

And nobody in my family is safe from this trolling for the sin of being related to me. My son, for instance. The Doctrine and Canon insists that we are not in contact with each other because he hates me. There is no room for the truth.

 William A. Ferguson follows

 Peter Schmalfeldt @mrmidi · Sep 17
@TheRealBobber @Support that is his pic. Here's the full one as proof. thecampofthesaints.files.wordpress.com/2013/02/bill-s... now please stop harassing me and my father.

💬 View conversation

Peter Schmalfeldt @mrmidi · Sep 17
@support the user @TheRealBobber seems to only harass my father. Their pic is my dad with Xs drawn over his eyes :(

 Bob Smallmind @TheRealBobber 23h
@DeepBrainTV it just KILLS you that you cant see the fun there, eh?

 Bob Smallmind @TheRealBobber 2d
@DeepBrainTV the projection, it BUUUURNS @wjjhoge

On Oct. 6, I posted a Tweet asking my various detractors to come up with a list of how I have injured them on a personal level. Crickets.

Oh wait. There was one from this very, very dim woman.

Back in May I filed a defamation lawsuit. I named this woman as a defendant. I withdrew the lawsuit a couple days later. But it affected the poor dear's blood pressure readings!

So evil am I!

LibraryGryffon
@LibraryGryffon

Does this picture look like your mother?

And no, Dim Girl, that looks nothing like my mother.

But I am happy you had no lasting ill-effects from the blood pressure problems that were no doubt caused by some evil spell I cast upon you, and nothing to do with a fondness for salty, fried food.

So then, back to the "wisdom" of "not feeding the trolls." The writer of "Trouble at the Koolaid Point" explains it like this.

THE GAME IS FIXED

I'm not sure I like comparing trolls to animals (because insulting to animals), but as an animal trainer, I'm painfully aware of the power of operant conditioning.

Yes, sure, "don't feed the trolls" has been the standard advice, a bullshit talking point propagated by trolls to blame their targets. "You brought this on. You don't want this? Don't engage." Except that's not actually true. It's the opposite of true, once you've been personally targeted.

As any parent of a two-year old can tell you, ignoring the child usually leads to escalation. Cry harder, scream louder, and in the most desperate scenarios, become destructive. Anything to get the attention they crave. Simply moving on is not an option for the haters once you've been labeled a Koolaid server and/or a rich source of lulz. Ignore them, and the trolls cry harder, scream louder, and become destructive.

If you've already hit the Koolaid Piont, you usually have just three choices:

1. leave (They Win)

2. ignore them (they escalate, make your life more miserable, DDoS, ruin your career, etc. i.e. They Win)

3. fight back (If you've already hit the Koolaid Point, see option #2. They Win).

That's right, in the world we've created, once you've become a Koolaid-point target they always win. Your life will never be the same, and the harassers will drain your scarce cognitive resources. You and your family will never be the same.

The hater trolls are looking for their next dopamine hit. If you don't provide it, they'll try harder. But the escalation to get a response from you? That's not even the worst escalation problem.

The more dangerous social-web-fueled gamification of trolling is the unofficial troll/hate leader-board. The attacks on you are often less about scoring points against you than that they're trying to out-do one another. They're trying to out-troll, out-hate, out-awful the other trolls. That's their ultimate goal. He who does the worst wins.

Which may explain the slow, steady increase in both frequency and horror of online harassment. What was mostly drive-by nasty comments in 2001 then progressed to Photoshopped images (your child on a porn image is a particularly "fun" one), and what's after images? Oh, yeah, the "beat up Anita" game. And what's left when you've done as much digital damage as you can?

Real-life damage.

Doxxing with calls to action (that — and trust me on this — people DO act on).

Swatting (look it up). That nobody has yet been killed in one of these "pranks" is surprising. It's just a matter of time.

Physical Assualt: the online attack on the epilepsy forums, where the trolls crafted flickering images at a frequency known to trigger seizures in those with "photosensitive" epilepsy. Think about this. People went to the one safe space they knew online — the epilepsy support forums — and found themselves having seizures before they could even look away. (Nobody was ever charged.)

Side note: I have epilepsy, though not the photosensitive kind. But I have a deep understanding of the horror of seizures, and the dramatically increased chance of death and brain damage many of us with epilepsy live with, in my case, since the age of 4. FYI, deaths related to epilepsy in the US are roughly equal with deaths from breast cancer. There isn't a shred of doubt in my mind that if the troll hackers could find a way to increase your risk of breast cancer? They'd do it. Because what's better than lulz? Lulz with BOOBS. Yeah, they'd do it.

But what disturbed me even more than the epilepsy forum attack itself were the comments about it afterwards (I won't link to it, but you can search for it on Wired). "I lol'd" "That's awful, but you gotta admit... hilarious!" Once again, high-fives all around. This is the world we have created.

So I don't have the luxury of assuming "it's just online. Not REAL. It's not like these people would ever do anything in the real world ." And what you don't hear much about is what most targeted women find the most frightening of all: the stalkerish energy, time, effort, focus on... YOU. The drive-by hate/threat comment, no matter how vile, is just that, a comment that took someone 2.5 seconds to think and execute. It might be annoying, offensive, maybe intimidating the first few times. But you get used to those, after all, it's not like somebody put time and effort into it.

But Photoshopped images? Stories drawn from your own work? There's a creepy and invasive horror knowing someone is pouring over your words, doing Google and Flickr image searches to find the perfect photo to manipulate. That someone is using their time and talent to write code even, about you. That's not trolling, that's obsession. That's the point where you know it's not really even about the Koolaid now…they're obsessed with you.

This is a very long way from the favorite troll talking point "Oh boohoo someone was mean on the internet."

Mean: "You're fat and retarded and deserve to be raped". (we all get tons of those, but those aren't what we're talking about)

Stalking: "Here's yet another creepy and terrifying thing I made for you and about you and notice just how much I know about you…" (1/200)

There is a difference.

We need to stop propagating the troll-driven meme that "it's all just trollin' and boohoo mean words you should cry more" and start making the hard, fine-grained distinctions. The hater trolls use the 'just trollin' and 'just mean words' to minimize even the worst attacks and gaslight their targets. In hater troll framing, there's no difference between a single tweet and a DDoS of your employer's website. There's no difference between a "you're a histrionic charlatan" and "here's a headless corpse and you are next and here's your address." It's all just trollin' and mean words and not real life.

It's all 'just trollin' unless you, you know, actually deserved it. Then they're all, "sure, things got a little out of hand, and threats of violence are never acceptable but, um, what did you expect?" Followed by, "Well actually, if it WERE actual HARASSMENT, then it's for The Authorities."

Fun Troll Logic:

```
IF no legal action happens THEN it
wasn't actually "real" harassment
```

You're probably more likely to win the lottery than to get any law enforcement agency in the United States to take action when you are harassed online, no matter how viscously and explicitly. Local agencies lack the resources, federal agencies won't bother. (Unless you're a huge important celebrity. But the rules are always different for them. But trolls are quite happy to attack people who lack the resources to do anything about it. Troll code totally supports punching DOWN.)

There IS no "the authorities" that will help us.

We are on our own.

And if we don't take care of one another, nobody else will.

We are all we've got.

Which brings me to why I really wrote this.

So, ignoring them doesn't work. Shutting down your Twitter timeline doesn't work. Fighting back doesn't work.

Does anything work?

3 NO. NOTHING WORKS.

There was a time when I was young and foolish and believed that the best way to shut down an anonymous Internet Troll was to strip away the layer of anonymity and shine the direct glare of the flashlight into their eyes.

This has worked in a few cases. But the majority of the people I've successfully identified just deny the fact that they've been identified. In other words, they lie.

Shocking, I know.

I am only going to name one formerly anonymous troll in this book, and that's because he continues to deny he is who he is, even though I have him dead to rights.

Meet Christopher S. Heather of Racine, Wisconsin.

BFF WITH GOV. WALKER!

Mr. Heather has been a thorn in my side since the aforementioned "Operation Burn Notice" days. Fact of the matter is, when the rest of the OBN knuckleheads realized that their work for Gov. Walker would come under closer scrutiny as he makes plans to run for President in 2016, the vast majority of them decided it was time to stop with the trolling and present themselves as adults who could be taken seriously, along with the candidate they support.

Not Chris Heather. Being an Internet Troll gave him a taste of power. For the first time in his life, Heather felt like a BIG MAN. This was a new drug for Heather, more intoxicating than the Bud Light one frequently sees him pictured with.

Chrissy likes a good time, young girls, a cold beer, fishing and his pals.

It must be doubly painful to Chrissy that it was some of his old "Operation Burn Notice" buddies that ratted him out to me.

"We told him to knock it off with the trolling," said a leader of the movement who we will call 'The Big Cheese."

"Everyone else was moving on with their lives but not Chris. He refused to rein himself in. Then, he turned on us. Knowing that he was still trolling you, we decided the only thing we could do was tell you his real name and let you take it from there."

So, I took it from there.

In early May, armed with the information provided by "The Big Cheese," I started my background check on the person who, until that time, I believed to be someone else, living in Arizona.

Every day, I learned a little more. But it wasn't enough. I needed something to definitely tie Chris Heather to the Twitter Wretch calling itself Embryriddlealum.

On May 18, 2014, I found it. And Heather gave himself away.

4 AH CHRISSY! VEE FOUND CHOO!

Here's how I reported the story on my blog, which no longer exists.

I Owe Robin Causey an Apology

Added by Bill Schmalfeldt on May 19, 2014.
Saved under Crazy Wingnuts, Top Stories

Here all this time, I believed he was the creature known as "Embryriddlealum." Every time I tried to broach the subject, he just took a smart ass tone like he was playing with me. But, I was wrong. I know who "Embryriddlealum" is, and he gave HIMSELF away! But first, I am not allowed to contact Robin. But if I could, I would apologize. This does not excuse his lying under oath on his Injunction Against Harassment, or that of his wife. But I was incorrect in labeling him as the vile and disgusting "Embryriddlealum."

I can tell you with 100 percent certainty that "Embryriddlealum" is none other than the same person who tweets as "Guntotingteabag" and God Knows How Many Other Sock Puppets. He is Christopher Heather of Racine, Wisconsin.

Follow me. You'll enjoy this.

I started to suspect I was wrong about Cause being ERA over the past several days. Even though he is a conservative scumbag and was involved in the Operation Burn Notice nonsense, I contacted one of the senior folks of the former Knot My Wisconsin group with whom I've developed a friendly relationship. He said he was aware of "Aaron Burr" who tweets as "SuperAaronBurr" and is, in fact, Robin Wesley Causey of Chino Valley, AZ. My new friend could not say for sure, but he was fairly certain that Heather was ERA.

So, I laid a little trapsy wapsy for ERA today. I did a search on the Wisconsin Judiciary Case Search and came up with a domestic violence case involving Chris Heather and a girl named Stacy Thomas. I've been taunting ERA with that all afternoon. He gave himself away when I said I had called her and she said the fight was because she made fun of his junk.

ERA, as idiots will do, gave himself away.

Howard Hanger-Earl @embryriddlealum · 58m
@wmsbroadcasting So you can talk to corpses now, Shake? You poor dumb bastard. You should come with a tuning key I play you so often...

Expand   ↩ Reply ⇄ Retweet ★ Favorite ••• More

Hah. So, he knows Stacy Thomas had shuffled off the mortal coil. Keep in mind, I did not mention Chris Heather at all in my taunting of ERA today. In fact, I covered his name on the Wisconsin report.

Filing Date	**Case Type**
03-10-1995	Civil
Class Code Description	**Responsible Official**
Domestic Abuse-Temp Rest Order	Kreul, Richard
Branch Id	
10	

Parties

Party Type	**Party Name**
Petitioner	
Respondent	Thomas, Stacy

The information contained in this report was compiled from thousands of local and national data public records databases to deliver the most comprehensive, accurate and up-to-date information available.

Name

Chris Heather

Age	Date of Birth	Phone Number
40	8/1973	262-639-9437

Additional Phone Numbers

262-639-2891

Most Recent Address

2830 Arlington Ave. Uppr, Racine, WI 53403-4208

So, where did Stacy Thomas live in 1995?

Contact Report
Stacy Thomas

Report Expiratio
November 19, 201

Name	Stacy Thomas
Age	Died in 2010 (35)
Date of Birth	2/26/1975
Phone Number	276-632-9430
Additional Phone Numbers	262-898-9999, 262-637-7092, 262-639-2889
Most Recent Address	2385 Stillmeadow Rd, Axton, VA 24054-3325
Aliases/Name Variations	Stacy L Thomas, Stacey L Thomas, S Thomas, Thomas Stacy

Email:

t****@yxxxx.cxx	**Stacy Thomas** 2385 Stillmeadow Rd Axton, VA 24054
k****@aol.com	**Stacy Thomas** 2385 Stillmeadow Rd Axton, VA 24054-3325
l****@juno.com	**Stacy Thomas** 2385 Stillmeadow Rd Axton, VA 24054-3325
s****@msn.com	**Stacy Thomas** 1316 Askin St Martinsville, VA 24112-4602

13 addresses were found

Address	City, State, Zip	Phone	Added	Updated
2385 Stillmeadow Rd	Axton, VA 24054-3325		1/2009	1/2009
1316 Askin St	Martinsville, VA 24112-4602	276-632-9430	3/2008	6/2008
2040 Quincy Ave, Apt 1	Racine, WI 53403-4233	262-898-9999	12/2005	12/2005
3116 Washington Ave	Racine, WI 53405-3050	xxx-639-2889	3/1998	3/1998
4122 Sheridan Rd	Mount Pleasant, WI 53403-3817		3/1995	3/1995
3155 Coolidge Ave	Mount Pleasant, WI 53403-3511		6/1993	6/1993

So...

A. Chris Heather got beat up by Stacy Thomas

B. I disguised Heather's name on the court report and accused ERA of getting beaten up by a girl.

C. ERA denied it all.

D. I told him I talked to her and she made fun of his penis size.

E. ERA says, "Oh, you can talk to corpses?" Meaning he knows she's dead.

F. A simple search finds Stacy L. Thomas, who once lived 5 miles away from Chris Heather, died in Virginia in 2010. She's the right age, or... was, I should say.

G. I never once mentioned the name "Chris Heather" in my taunt.

Therefore:

A+B+C+D+E+F+G=ERA is CHRIS HEATHER!

So, give it up, ERA. You, slimeball, are BUSTED!!!

To this day, Chris Heather denies he is Embryriddlealum. But when I pulled the trigger on him, he deleted this tweet from his timeline like it was poison.

 Howard Hanger-Earl @embryriddlealum · 58m
@wmsbroadcasting So you can talk to corpses now, Shake? You poor dumb bastard. You should come with a tuning key I play you so often...

Expand   ← Reply   ⇄ Retweet   ★ Favorite   ••• More

In my experience, when I am wrong about something, my target and his supporters tend to just let me be wrong. Heather has been squealing like a stuck hog ever since his real identity has been revealed.

And now that I have turned him in to law enforcement for the death threat, he's squealing even louder.

Do I expect anything to come of my turning him in to the cops? Do I think they'll bother with an investigation or anything so time-consuming or costly as that?

What do you think?

5 CALL THE POL… MEH, NEVER MIND

When an individual in Westminster, Maryland brought me up on 367 unfounded misdemeanor charges that were dropped by the state's attorney's office, I asked for an investigation.

None was forthcoming.

When another troll began writing false reviews about books I've written, books he's never purchased or read, I reported him to his local cops and was told what he was doing was not illegal.

Now that there is an extant (in my opinion) death threat against me, I have attempted to invoke police protection.

Wanna guess the results so far?

To whoever is reading this.

I received the latest in what I consider to be a legitimate death threat from a Racine County, Wisconsin, resident.

His name is **Christopher S. Heather. He lives at [redacted]** For more than two years, ever since 2012, in my role as an investigative reporter and I busted up his "Operation Burn Notice" scheme where he and several chums were engaged in pretending to gather recall petitions in the Governor's recall election in Wisconsin, then destroying them instead of turning them in, Mr. Heather has been sending me harassing images. Mostly calling on my to commit suicide

Chris Heather and Gov.Scott Walker (R-WI)

I think he's gotten tired of waiting.

 Howard D. Earl (@embryriddlealum)   October 4, 2014 at 10:40 am

👍 2 👎 0 🔄 Rate This

You poor dumb bastard (literally), Shakey. You are too dumb and far too obtuse to ever realize that you have never posted a pic that has anything to do with me. You have no idea who I am. You have never even been close.

You will know who I am on your death bed. I will make sure of it. And hopefully it will be soon.

Reply

 Howard D. Earl (@embryriddlealum)   October 4, 2014 at 10:45 am

👍 1 👎 0 🔄 Rate This

I will take it upon myself now, to post the most vile photos, of every one of Bill Schmalfeldt's family members.

Did your mom ever blow a donkey?

Did your dad service Muslim prisoners?

Does Gail work Balmer street corners?

Photographic proof coming soon.Because I know who THEY are.

Be looking for my new wordpress site.

But by all means, keep doing what you're doing.

Reply

More about my parents and wife later.

Here are some of the images sent directly to me via Twitter and Facebook over the past two years by this individual.

 Operation Burn Notice
This hour is brought to you by the CURE FOR PARKINSON'S DISEASE.

 Like · Comment · Share · Sunday at 2:58pm ·

👍 5 people like this.

 **Howard D. Earl**
@embryriddlealum

 Follow

@DeepBrainRadio @antvq16 @guntotingteabag The cure, Shaky. THE CURE!

↩ Reply   ↻ Retweet   ★ Favorite   ••• More

8:07 AM - 2 Dec 2013

Howard D. Earl @embryriddlealum · Nov 13
@guntotingteabag **The CURE**

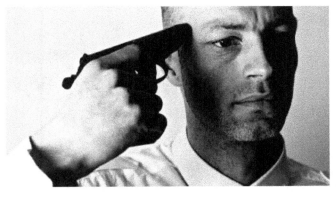

View more photos and videos

I have Stage IV Parkinson's disease. I can not walk without assistance. Mr. Heather finds this quite humorous.

He also enjoys taunting me over the death of my mother in

2013 and my father in 1983.

Howard D. Earl
@embryriddlealum

I'm 100% positive. No doubt, whatsoever that I am NOT Jerry Fletcher or Robin Causey. Pointer and Laugher at Inspector Jiggles Enterprises.

That is my mom's face with the X over the eyes, photoshopped to a Jesus with a Rifle photo.

46

Shaky McSpittle
@ParkinsonsHumor

TWEETS
159

That is my Mom with a Star Trek Monster over her face.
Here is the original photo

This is my father, who died in 1983 at 54 from pancreatic
cancer.

Howard D. Earl @embryriddlealum · May 3
@guntotingteabag @palatinepundit @brainsrfood I found a pic of his dad, too.
↰ Reply ⇄ Retweet ★ Favorite

My wife, Gail, had cancer a couple years ago. Happy to say, she seems to have beaten it. But she tripped and fell the other day. Heather is making it seem like I'm a wife beater by taking a photo from a website about her recovery and altering the photo.

disagreement?--> @BlitzParkinsons <-- @CoulsonJason @mayberryville

View conversation

 Howard D. Earl @embryriddlealum · Sep 30

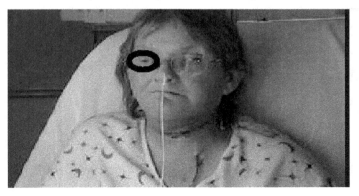

TWEETS

26

Gayle Smallfield

@captivenurse

Trapped by one bad decision

Another Chris Heather website.

49

William A. Ferguson follows

Peter Schmalfeldt @mrmidi · Sep 17
@TheRealBobber @Support that is his pic. Here's the full one as proof.
thecampofthesaints.files.wordpress.com/2013/02/bill-s... now please stop
harassing me and my father.

View conversation

Peter Schmalfeldt @mrmidi · Sep 17
@support the user @TheRealBobber seems to only harass my father. Their pic
is my dad with Xs drawn over his eyes :(

Bob Smallmind @TheRealBobber   23h
@DeepBrainTV it just KILLS you that
you cant see the fun there, eh?

Bob Smallmind @TheRealBobber   2d
@DeepBrainTV the projection, it
BUUUURNS @wjjhoge

He even harasses my son in St. Louis with another of his
websites. His avatar is my head after surgery for Parkinson's
disease.

I identified this man as Chris Heather when his former
Operation Burn Notice associate [redacted] gave me his
name. [Redacted] is a good enough guy, and he told me
who it was that had been harassing me over the years. They
had fun with the pretend "Operation Burn Notice" thing, but
time came to grow up when they realized Gov. Walker was
considering a 2016 run. Everybody cleaned up, lost weight,
became respectable, except for Chris Heather who wanted
to continue the flame wars. When he ignored their warnings
to cease and desist, [Redcted] notified me about the man's
identity, which I ascertained on my own by setting a trap for
him that he fell right into, giving himself away.

Troopers, I have presented this info to Racine authorities. They say I have to contact local authorities. I contacted local authorities in the Howard Count Sheriff's Office, Police Department and the State's Attorney's office. No response. If I can't get a response from the Maryland State Police, then I am going to have to go further up the food chain.

As I said, <u>I am a Stage IV Parkinson's Patient</u>. I retired from the federal government as a GS-13 Writer Editor with the National Institutes of Health in 2011. I have had this illness for 14 years. This ended a 30+ year career in broadcasting and journalism. I am incapable of self defense. I need protection. I do not want to be one of those people who asked for help and nobody did anything until it was too late. And frankly, this man scares the bejeezus out of me.

If there's nothing the Maryland State Police can do to contact the Wisconsin authorities and get them investigating Mr. Heather, then please advise me what my next steps should be. He is ratcheting up his threats on blog comments and on Twitter, and frankly he strikes me as a dangerous, unstable person who is a danger to me, to Wisconsin Democratic Gubernatorial Candidate Mary Burke, and anyone else who crosses his path. He is well armed and brags about it.

Can you help me?

Nobody expects immediate results. But so far? Crickets.

The author of "Trouble at the Koolaid Point" writes about the difficulty of getting law enforcement interested in the threats being made against you as a victim of Internet Trolling.

WHY I CAME BACK

Most of the back-story is not important, and I hope to never have to talk about it again, but here's the relevant bits:

In 2007, I was the target of a several-week long escalating harassment campaign that culminated in my being doxxed (a word I didn't even know then) with a long, detailed, explicit document, posted pretty much everyone on the internet (including multiple times to my own wikipedia entry). It was a sort of open letter with a sordid (but mostly fictional) account that included my past, my career, my family, and wrapped up with my (unfortunately NOT fictional) social security number, former home address and, worst of all — a call to action for people to send things to me. They did. I never returned to my blog, I cut out almost all speaking engagements, and rarely appeared anywhere in the tech world online or real world. Basically, that was it for me. I had no desire then to find out what comes after doxxing, especially not with a family, and I had every reason to believe this would continue to escalate if I didn't, well, stop "serving the Koolaid."

A year later, I had one of the worst days of my life. I got a phone call from a journalist, Mattathias Schwartz. He'd been working on a long-form feature magazine story about trolls for the NY Times, and it was about to come out. He wanted to warn me about something in the story, something nobody expected: one of the main subjects of his story had just — out of the blue — announced that he was "Memphis Two" the author of That Document (i.e. my dox) and added that he was part of the harassment of Kathy Sierra.

I sat down. "I've never heard of this person. Am I in any danger?" He gave me the only truthful answer, "I don't know." But then he added, "I don't think so, because honestly I don't think he sees you as important at all." So, whew. He was right. I was not important. And after all, they'd already put checkmark in the WIN column for me. I was gone. I'd not be serving any more Koolaid. Nothing to see here, etc.

And there I hoped it would end, fading away as all things do as the internet moves on and this troll I'd never heard of would just go back to whatever it was that trolls do.

But you all know what happened next. Something something something horrifically unfair government case against him and just like that, he becomes tech's "hacktivist hero." He now had A Platform not just in the hacker/troll world but in the broader tech community I was part of. And we're not just talking stories and interviews in Tech Crunch and HuffPo (and everywhere else), but his own essays in those publications. A tech industry award. His status was elevated, his reach was broadened. And for reasons I will never understand, he suddenly had gained not just status and Important Friends, but also "credibility".

Did not see that coming.

But hard as I tried to find a ray of hope that the case against him was, somehow, justified and that he deserved, somehow, to be in prison for this, oh god I could not find it. I could not escape my own realization that the cast against him was wrong. So wrong. And not just wrong, but wrong in a way that puts us all at risk. I wasn't just angry about the injustice of his case, I had even begun to feel sorry for him. Him. The guy who hates me for lulz. Guy who nearly ruined my life. But somehow, even I had started to buy into his PR. That's just how good the spin was. Even I mistook the sociopath for a misunderstood outcast. Which, I mean, I actually knew better.

And of course I said nothing until his case was prosecuted and he'd been convicted, and there was no longer anything I could possibly do to hurt his case. A small group of people — including several of his other personal victims (who I cannot name, obviously) asked me to write to the judge before his sentencing, to throw my weight/story into the "more reasons why weev should be sent to prison". I did not. Last time, for the record, I did NOTHING but support weev's case, and did not speak out until after he'd been convicted.

But the side-effect of so many good people supporting his case was that more and more people in tech came to also… like him. And they all seemed to think that it was All Good as long as they punctuated each article with the obligatory "sure, he's an ass" or "and yes, he's a troll" or "he's known for offending people" (which are, for most men, compliments). In other words, they took the Worst Possible Person, as one headline read, and still managed to reposition him as merely a prankster, a trickster, a rascal. And who doesn't like a "lovable scoundrel"?

So I came back because I saw what was happening.

I came back because I connected these dots:

* Weev writes an explicit warning to all women in tech that speaking out (in his words "squealing like a stuck pig") will be "punished".

* Weev demonstrates this by punishing a woman that was, for better or worse, a role model for some in the already-way-too-small group of women in tech.

* Weev then becomes celebrated in tech, spun as a straight-talking, no bullshit, asshole who speaks truth to power. Truth. Weev. Is. About. Truth. And Privacy. Ours. He wanted to protect Our Privacy with The Truth.

(If you want an example of gaslighting, imagine how I felt watching this unfold)

* And there it is. I came because if weev is credible, and endorsed as a "friend", then the document he, at the least, ENTHUSIASTICALLY CONTINUES TO ENDORSE, is... well what does this mean?

I came back because I believe this sent a terrible, devastating message about what was acceptable. Because nobody in a position of power and influence in the tech world ever, NOT ONCE, brought up the explicit threats in that document, except for The Verge. (Tim Carmody, Greg Sandoval, you are my heroes).

I came back and watched endless streams of funny, casual, online banter between weev and some of those I respected and trusted most in tech. You know who I mean. I watched him being retweeted into my stream in a positive way. I actually did lol, though, when Twitter's algorithm kept insisting You Probably Want To Follow Him! That's how much our Venn diagrams overlapped.

But the one thing I never expected was that after all these years, he'd suddenly deny it. Even more so, that reasonable, logical, intelligent people would actually believe this. He'd suddenly, after 6 years, claim that a world-class, international, Livingston-winner ("Pulitzer of the Young") journalist would just somehow… come up with that. And that in six years it never occurred to weev, not once, to publicly deny it no matter how many times he was asked about it.

(Schwartz himself came into these conversations more than once over the past year to remind weev about their conversation, to confirm that yes, it happened exactly as he described in the 2008 feature. Not that it made a difference. After all, in weev vs. amazing writer with everything to lose by lying, who are you going with? Weev. They went with weev.)

As I said in a now-deleted Twitter exchange, I couldn't imagine "what sort of suspension of disbelief" one needs to accept a context in which a journalist who has never heard of me, somehow pulls MY name and that document out of thin air, then somehow mistakenly attributes it to the object of his story. Or that why, in all those years, weev never once publicly tried to refute this? He even wrote a response to the NYTimes story (the story where he outs himself as the doxxer) on his own blog, where he takes issue with several aspects of the article but never disputes the facts, and never even hints that weev-as-my-doxxer was inaccurate.

And he's been asked about it many times over the next years, including that GQ interview where he explained his reasons for doing it. Never once, until I returned, did he ever publicly deny it. The NYTimes article stands, for 6 years, without correction or challenges. Weev of course now claims he wrote to the NYTimes, but has never produced, you know, "evidence".

So there I was, now having unbelievable conversations with prominent people in tech that were more willing to believe the most absurd story over, well, one of the most respected journalists still left in the world. That they were willing to believe weev over... common sense. Logic. That they had the fantasy belief that though weev was known to be one of the most skillful and manipulative liars (and that description is from a friend of his), somehow, he wasn't lying now, to them. I pushed back, but only if it was someone in the tech world who was not a troll, but an intelligent, rational, reasonable, person.

I underestimated the willingness of people to still, no matter what, believe him.

But recently I came to realize that OK let's say we do suspend disbelief and let's say he didn't do it. Let's say he simply wanted people to think he'd done it. That doesn't actually change it.

Because the problem, the reason I came back is this:

Weev unequivocally, enthusiastically, gleefully, repeatedly ENDORSED it. He tweeted, many times, that I "had it coming". I deserved it. That the "truth" in my dox was why I left the internet the first time.

And so again, I connect these dots:

* A document issues an explicit threat, warning women against speaking out. Lots and lots of women in tech have seen this document.

* Weev endorses this document, enthusiastically, repeatedly.

* Prominent people in tech endorse weev

Which could easily be seen as…

* Prominent people in tech tacitly endorsed that threat against speaking out.

Some of those people are/were feminists. I cannot even comprehend the cognitive dissonance.

THAT's why I wanted to push back. Every. Single. Time. If someone described me, or the article about me as a lie, (as @erratarob did on my last day) I stepped in to do what I thought was the most rational approach: to just keep pointing to the facts that were known. To push back on the twist and spin. I believed the fine-grained distinctions mattered. I pushed back because I believed I was pushing back on the implicit message that women would be punished for speaking out. I pushed back because almost nobody else was, and it seemed like so many people in tech were basically OK with that.

But a few days ago, in the middle of one of those "discussions", this time with @erratarob, I realized it wasn't worth it. He concluded that I was just trolling so people would troll me back. I asked him what he thought I should have done. And his answer was "don't feed the trolls." "Ignore it and move on." Perhaps Rob didn't know that I'd already tried that for six years, but that it was weev who kept that damn thing alive no matter how gone I was. He managed to tweet to my social security number not long before he went to prison, and well before I resurfaced. No, I didn't troll him into that. I didn't "engage".

But Rob didn't do anything wrong. He was saying what he truly believes. What, sadly, a whole lot of people in tech believe. Rob just happened to be the last "you asked for it" message I wanted to hear. So I just stopped.

I didn't "rage quit", I just walked away. I shut off a big cognitive resource leak. From the beginning of my time tweeting as Seriouspony, that I tweeted I was not likely to stay and that I was looking forward to where we would end up next. I'm not GONE gone. I'm just not on Twitter. But I have to add I'm surprised to see my leaving Twitter as, once again, an example of someone who "just shouldn't be on the internet". Because nothing says "unbalanced" like having the freedom to walk away from a social media network. Because you can. Because you have a choice. Because you have the most beautiful and awesome ponies on the planet.

So, how did I find myself involved with these vile trolls in the first place?

Glad you asked. It's quite a story.

6 BECAUSE I HAD AN OPINION THEY DIDN'T LIKE – THAT'S WHY!

Two of these people, dead before their time, are used by Republicans to raise a lot of money. One was killed by a Republican. Nobody raises a cent for that one.

The victim had every reason to believe there was a long, successful life ahead. Seated in the car, there was no reason to worry, no way to know that death was just seconds away. When the victim was eventually taken to the morgue, there was talk that the death was not accidental. But the killer was never charged in the untimely death of someone so young, someone whose life held so much promise.

Laura Welch never had to answer for killing her former boyfriend, 17-year old Michael Douglas, t-boning his car when she sped past a stop sign on a clear, Texas night, throwing Douglas from his car, breaking his neck, killing him instantly.

No, Laura never had to answer for the death. She married a young oil baron whose main goal in life was owning a baseball team. His name was George W. Bush.

Bring up Laura Bush's role in the death of young Michael Douglas, conservatives bubble over with reasons why she should not be held to blame.

Carl DeLong, however, had the bad luck of seeing a gym bag that had a bomb in it. He went to pick it up. It exploded, tearing off one of his legs, amputating two fingers. Brett Kimberlin had never met Carl Delong. He was convicted for a series of bombings in Speedway, Indiana in the 1970s, along with other crimes, and went to prison. He has since been paroled and works for social justice with an organization called the Justice Through Music Project. And he can never, never, NEVER be forgiven for killing a man that he did not kill. Never mind that most of the people who hate Kimberlin with a white-hot passion would never recognize Carl DeLong if they were alone in an elevator with him. They would be able to tell you NOTHING about the man, save for the oft-repeated "he was a Vietnam vet" as if that meant something to a generation of right wingers who avoided military service like dogs avoid stepping in their own poop.

Carl DeLong is the Breitbart generation's version of Mary Jo Kopechne. After all the social good Senator Teddy Kennedy did for America, for the less fortunate, for those who were disenfranchised by society, Kennedy's death was greeted with glad tidings by Andrew Breitbart and his supporters. You would think they knew Mary Jo Kopechne personally, and that Kennedy had held her head under water until the bubbles stopped, instead of making several panicked attempts to find her in the dark water before giving up. His handlers kept him from police until he could pass a breathalyzer.

Nobody bothered to check Laura Welch for alcohol in 1963.

Breitbart's survivors use the image of Carl DeLong just like Kennedy haters used Miss Kopechne. Even though DeLong took his own life five years after the explosion that maimed him, they blame his death on Kimberlin. Just like Kopechne gave the right wing sufficient justification to hate Kennedy, even though they wouldn't be able to tell you a detail of the girl's life, Kimberlin's detractors use DeLong's suicide as justification to hate Kimberlin and to declare him guilty of crimes he was never even charged with, let alone convicted of.

The reason is simple, of course. Teddy Kennedy was a fund raising godsend for the right wing. All the right wing organizations had to do was send out mailers reminding people of the young girl Teddy "murdered" in his car that night in 1969 and the money flowed like wine.

The lesson was not lost on Aaron Walker, R. Stacy McCain, Patrick Frey, Mandy Nagy, Lee Stranahan, Ali Akbar, and the others connected to them who continue to use Brett Kimberlin as a modern day Freddy Kruger... lurking around every corner, skulking in every bush. Waiting to strike again, to kill without mercy.

Kimberlin wanted to know the name of an anonymous lawyer assisting someone in a nuisance lawsuit. He learned that Aaron Worthing was actually attorney Aaron Walker, author of the "Everyone Draw Mohammed Day" blog. This being revealed amounted to a death threat. You can raise money from a death threat.

When R. Stacy McCain alleged that Kimberlin called McCain's wife's employer to see if there was some way the employer could get McCain off his back, that turned into another death threat in which McCain took to the breeze, leaving his wife and kids behind in Hagerstown (he says) to protect them, because if he wasn't there then he was free to keep writing about this ravenous wolf in human skin known as Kimberlin who certainly would never even think of murdering McCain's wife and piglets if Papa Pig wasn't home. He raised a lot of money on that.

In fact, on a smaller scale, Kimberlin has been a cash cow for these Breitbart remnants like Kennedy was for the Republican party. If you do a search for ALL the names, Brett Kimberlin, R. Stacy McCain, Patrick Frey or Patterico, Mandy Nagy, Aaron Worthing, Lee Stranahan and Ali Akbar… put all those names in quotes in a Google search bar. 1,320 hits. 1,320 web sites where McCain and Frey and Nagy and Worthing and Akbar and Stranahan are in fear of their lives and asking readers to send them money. For God's sake, only YOUR DONATIONS will allow them to stay alive long enough to continue the fight against this monster who has hurt no one, damaged no property, and has lived a blameless life since his parole in 2001. McCain, Frey, Nagy, Worthing, Akbar, Stranahan, et. al., NEED you to be AFRAID that Brett Kimberlin is in the bushes outside YOUR house, lurking in the dark, holding a bomb… waiting. Just waiting. And only they can keep you safe, but they will need your money to do it. Beats working for a living.

7 MY BODY OF WORK ON THE SUBJECT OF ANAL RAPE AND THE ENJOYMENT THEREOF

There has been more written and published in these clippings from Google about what a horrible anal rape enthusiast (meaning, that I am horrible and an anal rape enthusiast, not that I'm horrible at BEING an anal rape enthusiast) than I ever wrote on the subject.

First, the clippings.

Dishonest Bill Schmalfeldt Got Banned from Daily Kos for ...
theothermccain.com/.../dishonest-bill-schmalfeldt-got-banned-from-daily... ▾
Feb 20, 2013 - To say that Schmalfeldt's graphic discussion of what he called "the Butt Stuff" was obscene and offensive is to understate the matter. Perhaps ...

Bill Schmalfeldt: Sadism, Sodomy and Other Bizarre Mental ...
theothermccain.com/.../bill-schmalfeldt-sadism-sodomy-and-other-bizarr... ▾
Sep 30, 2013 - "It's the 'Butt Stuff.' . . . "Male conservatives are convinced that gay men want to put their ying yangs in THEIR BUTTS! This is a horrifying ...

Jeff Dunetz on Twitter: "RT @rsmccain: It's the "Butt Stuff ...
https://twitter.com/yidwithlid/status/384853946839605251 ▾
Sep 30, 2013 - ... Unfollow Blocked Unblock Pending Cancel. Jeff Dunetz @yidwithlid Sep 30. RT @rsmccain: It's the "Butt Stuff," Bill Schmalfeldt explained ...

Robert Stacy McCain on Twitter: ""It's the 'butt stuff.' ..." -- Bi...
https://twitter.com/rsmccain/status/430799058240679936 ▾
Feb 4, 2014 - ... Blocked Unblock Pending Cancel. Robert Stacy McCain @rsmccain Feb 4. "It's the 'butt stuff.' ..." -- Bill Schmalfeldt, banned from Daily Kos ...

Bill **Schmalfeldt**: Too Disgusting For Daily Kos | Lee Stranahan

leestranahan.com/bill-**schmalfeldt**-too-disgusting-for-daily-kos/ ▾

Nov 25, 2012 - R.S. McCain has been putting the career of Bill **Schmalfeldt** into proper perspective over at The Other McCain and it felt it was time to highlight ...

anal rape | Running Wolf

runwolf.wordpress.com/tag/**anal-rape**/ ▾

Jul 7, 2014 - Here's what **Schmalfeldt** had to say. I don't understand your obsession with **anal rape**. - Bill **Schmalfeldt** in an approved comment on this blog.

Kyle Kiernan on Twitter: @rsmccain **Schmalfeldt** is an **anal** ...

https://twitter.com/kylekiernan/status/397039899955585024 ▾

Nov 3, 2013 - @rsmccain **Schmalfeldt** is an **anal rape** enthusiast which he learned one day when he mispoked. Reply; Retweet Retweeted; Favorite ...

The Man Revisits - Different Day, Same Shit. - Blogger

macklyons.blogspot.com/2013/.../the-man-revisits-true-reasons-why.htm... ▾

Apr 6, 2013 - Instead of a mea culpa, **Schmalfeldt** wrote another post that politely told ... that **Schmalfeldt's** graphic discussion of what he called "**the Butt Stuff**" ...

Who's obsessed with what? | Running Wolf

runwolf.wordpress.com/2014/07/07/whos-obsessed-with-what/ ▾

Jul 7, 2014 - Bill **Schmalfeldt** decided to accuse your host of something rather vile and ... to calling "**the butt stuff**," including his infamous anal rape "fantasy.".

The Man Revisits - Different Day, Same Shit. - Blogger

macklyons.blogspot.com/2013/.../the-man-revisits-true-reasons-why.htm... ▾

Apr 6, 2013 - Instead of a mea culpa, **Schmalfeldt** wrote another post that politely told ... that **Schmalfeldt's** graphic discussion of what he called "**the Butt Stuff**" ...

Who's obsessed with what? | Running Wolf

runwolf.wordpress.com/2014/07/07/whos-obsessed-with-what/ ▾

Jul 7, 2014 - Bill **Schmalfeldt** decided to accuse your host of something rather vile and ... to calling "**the butt stuff**," including his infamous anal rape "fantasy.".

Humor | The Thinking Man's Zombie | Page 2

https://thinkingmanszombie.wordpress.com/category/humor/page/2/ ▾

Jun 3, 2014 - ... if I wasn't being included, because you know how I loves **the BUTT STUFF**. .... **Schmalfeldt** Wants To Be 'Shut Down,' Not Argued With.

In Re ELH-14-CV-1683 | hogewash

hogewash.com/2014/06/26/in-re-elh-14-cv-1683-5/

Jun 26, 2014 - A side note: **Schmalfeldt** was accompanied to court by Brett ..... "Vile and filthy" from the keyboard of the font from which "**the butt stuff**" flows?

Hashtag - #HoCoMD

www.totally.me/hashtagtrends/instagramtrends2013/hashtag/HoCoMD ▾
May 4, 2014 - Deranged Cyberstalker Bill **Schmalfeldt** 's Obscenity in #HoCoMD .... #
ElkridgeMD's **Anal Rape** Enthusiast/Troll Bill **Schmalfeldt** Violates Peace ...

Popehat - Part 15

www.popehat.com/page/15/ ▾ Pope Hat ▾
Nov 9, 2013 - For instance: today Bill **Schmalfeldt** made what I interpret as a public ....
digital **anal rape** of a citizen by government employees, commenter

And Now, Helpless Victim Bill **Schmalfeldt** Heroically Suffers ...

www.allthingsnow.com/.../And+Now,+Helpless+Victim+Bill+**Schmalfeldt**... ▾
Feb 21, 2013 - Bill **Schmalfeldt**: Not cropped to 'look positively demonic' .... Dishonest
Bill **Schmalfeldt** Got Banned from Daily Kos for **Anal Rape** 'Satire'; Feb.

The Other McCain » The Kimberlin Files - Rssing.com

kimberlin61.rssing.com/chan-7094138/all_p2.html ▾
04/06/13--17:55: Bill **Schmalfeldt's** Very Bad Idea UPDATE: Maryland Resident .... he
got banned from Daily Kos for a genuinely disgusting rant about **anal rape**.

Disqus – Phineas T. Barnum

disqus.com/phineastbarnum/ ▾
Deranged Cyberstalker Bill **Schmalfeldt** Continues His Obsessive Cyberstalking ...
Dishonest Bill **Schmalfeldt** Got Banned from Daily Kos for **Anal Rape** 'Satire'.

Prevarication Du Jour | hogewash

hogewash.com/2014/07/15/prevarication-du-jour-102/ ▾
Jul 15, 2014 - The Dreadful Pro-Se **Schmalfeldt**™ is now trying to spin a story of
WordPress taking ... Writes quaint mock-radio scripts v. writes **anal rape** porn.

32 thoughts on "Prevarication Du Jour" - Hogewash

hogewash.com/2013/11/03/prevarication-du-jour-28/
Nov 3, 2013 - Bill **Schmalfeldt** has, of course, guessed wrong. He is making an ... 2013
at 20:34 said: His **anal rape** "satire" is coming back to haunt him...

Team Kimberlin Post of the Day | hogewash

hogewash.com/2014/07/27/team-kimberlin-post-of-the-day-515/ ▾
Jul 27, 2014 - Like the rest of Team Kimberlin, The Dreadful Pro-Se **Schmalfeldt**™ is a
... v. kicked-off-KOS-for-publishing-his-**anal-rape**-fantasy, and fired from ...

Bill **Schmalfeldt** Lies to @SilverbergDave: Failure and the ...

deadcitizensrightssociety.wordpress.com/.../bill-**schmalfeldt**-lies-to-silver... ▾
Oct 31, 2013 - Bill **Schmalfeldt** has a habit of getting himself banned. He got banned
from Daily Kos because of his grossly offensive **anal rape** "satire," and ...

And now, let's take a moment to enjoy ever word I've ever written on the subject of "The Butt Stuff" as they call it.

So, it's not anal sex (as a practice) to which these small, frightened men object.

Heck, if you're a man and you're honest with yourself, you LIKE being on the "doling it out" *end of anal sex. How many heterosexual men reading this diary right now have never asked their wife or girlfriend to just take a deep breath, relax,* "I'll just put in the tip and we'll see how it goes," *and then you ram it home like Captain Kidd jamming his sword back into his scabbard while she hollers* "takeitouttakeitouttakeitout" *and you tell her to just relax and it won't hurt so bad and she starts kicking and screaming* "takeitOUTtakeitOUTtakeitOUT youfuckingbastardpieceofshit" *and you finally do* (because the walls are thin and your neighbors just LOVE calling the cops) *and you tell her she should have at least given herself a chance to relax and enjoy it and she (if she's your wife) doesn't let you anywhere near her with* "that thing" *for weeks and if she's your girlfriend she stops returning your calls?*

My career as an anal rape enthusiast lasted for 175 words. Now let's look at the entire Daily Kos column, in context, as intended as a screed against stupid conservative heterosexual men who have no problem with girl-o-girl homosexuality as long as the women are gorgeous and wearing high heeled shoes, but the very idea of man-on-man action makes them sick.

My friends at <u>Little Green Footballs</u> step forward today with a compelling, scholarly article about why Conservatives fear gay marriage. If I may borrow a paragraph?

Could this be the correct explanation of the fear? Could it be that conservatives (subconsciously?) believe that if same-sex marriage were to become more accepted and hence more common, heterosexuals would actually begin converting their sexual orientation? Could conservatives really (subconsciously?) believe that gay sex is so much better than straight sex, or that switching one's sexual preference is, at least for most people, as easy as switching brands? It sounds silly, but you do often hear conservatives fantasizing about gay folks - especially teachers - "recruiting" children who would otherwise be straight, as if changing or determining someone's sexual orientation - even a child's - were as easy as giving them the right sales pitch!

As usual, the good folks at LGF are on to something. But I say the reasons why Conservatives -- especially MALE conservatives -- have such dread of gay marriage are much more simple and selfish.

It's the "Butt Stuff."

(Allow me to explain after the leap.)

Male conservatives are convinced that gay men want to put their ying yangs in THEIR BUTTS! This is a horrifying prospect to your average, stupid male. This is why a blanket recognition that being gay is a normal variant of human sexuality, to these small, frightened, uneducated men, means society is saying it's OK for these gay men to put their willy-wallys in YOUR pooter hole!

Follow the logic.

Most stupid men, married or otherwise, enjoy pornography. They enjoy watching men with their throbbing, erect whatchamacallits do degrading thing to women with them. Slapping them on the face with it. Spanking them with it. There is no orifice on a woman's body that is safe from the probing, pulsating prongs on the popular pornos. And that includes the pooter hole. There's a whole SUBSET of pornography DEVOTED to anal sex. They give an AWARD at the ADULT VIDEO AWARDS each year to the actress involved in the most erotic Anal Sex scene.

So, it's not anal sex (as a practice) to which these small, frightened men object.

Heck, if you're a man and you're honest with yourself, you LIKE being on the "doling it out" end of anal sex. How many heterosexual men reading this diary right now have never asked their wife or girlfriend to just take a deep breath, relax, "I'll just put in the tip and we'll see how it goes," and then you ram it home like Captain Kidd jamming his sword back into his scabbard while she hollers "takeitouttakeitouttakeitout" and you tell her to just relax and it won't hurt so bad and she starts kicking and screaming "takeitOUTtakeitOUTtakeitOUT youfuckingbastardpieceofshit" and you finally do (because the walls are thin and your neighbors just LOVE calling the cops) and you tell her she should have at least given herself a chance to relax and enjoy it and she (if she's your wife) doesn't let you anywhere near her with "that thing" for weeks and if she's your girlfriend she stops returning your calls?

So. We've established we have no problem with the theory of anal sex. Or the theory of oral sex, for that matter. If you're clean and perform proper hygienic maintenance "down there", most women will be more than happy from time to time to engage in this particular activity. And fellows, you know that this is a two way street, right? T'is well and good to give and receive.

So, no problem with oral sex.

Same sex? Shoot, that's fine too! As long as it's woman on woman.

This is as old as time itself. Why do you think the Bible not only authorizes but condones multiple wives for the biblical patriarchs? Because after a hard day of patriarching, there's nothing a patriarch likes better than to come home to watch some hot "wife on wife" action (they didn't have Blu-Ray or DVDs then) before jumping into the wife pile.

Now, with our modern technology, we love watching the ladies do other ladies. If you are married or in a relationship and your wife or girlfriend comes home with an attractive friend, and says "Happy Birthday, honey" as she and her friend peel off their clothes revealing their Victoria's Secret scanties as they hop onto the bed and start kissing and fooling around for awhile before beckoning you to join them, would you throw your hands up in Conservative horror and quote Leviticus? NO! You'd be on that bed, living the dream! Oh HAPPY day! What a HAPPY day!

So. Let's review. It's not anal sex as a practice that we find loathsome. Nor is it oral sex. Same sex is not a problem either, as long as those same sexes happen to be two or more women.

(Ever wonder why the Bible never condoned a woman having more than one husband? I think it was comedian Wanda Sykes who asked if anyone had ever come home from work to find his wife watching a man-on-man porno saying, "Yeah, baby. Ooooh. He likes that, doesn't he? Oh, yeah, baby. Give it to him!")

Therefore, if the Conservative male has no problem with anal sex, oral sex or same sex sex, why the problem with Gay Marriage?

It can't be the reason they constantly give,"because it threatens the sanctity of marriage."

I've been married three times. My wife #3 and I have been together since 1988. The first two failed because I was married to women who couldn't keep their pants on when I was not around. "Teh Gay" had nothing to do with it.

So, the real reason people are against Gay Marriage comes down to one of two things.

1. You are a closeted homosexual, self-loathing, raised in a household that forbade and punished "those kinds of thoughts". You have repressed these feelings, have gotten married and have children but can only find real sexual satisfaction with the kind of anonymous sex initiated with a game of "tappy toe" in a Minneapolis Airport Bathroom. Or,

2. You are ignorant heterosexual who -- because YOU would gladly fuck a warm piece of liver if no one was looking -- believes that all gay men will find YOU attractive and want to force their sexual attentions on YOU! Men over 40 don't even like going to the doctor because they know the doc will stick a well-lubricated, gloved finger "up there." The idea of being run to ground by hoards of pantless gay men with their throbbing manhoods acting like divining wands in the search for "virgin ass" terrifies you. And you KNOW that's the next step. You KNOW that's what gays REALLY want... not monogamous relationships with people they love. Hell, YOU have a monogamous relationship with someone YOU love and yet every time you go out of town on a business trip you're balls deep in some hooker you met on Craigslist by 11:13 pm!
That's why you're against gays in the military. All gays want to have sex with YOU! You just KNOW it. So if you were in the Army and had to take a shower with GAY people looking at you, it would be a constant battle to maintain your anal virginity. If you were in a FOXHOLE (God forbid) with a GAY, then nobody

would be securing the perimeter because you would be too busy securing your ANUS against this GAY guy who you just KNOW wants to fuck you. Oh sure, he's sitting over there nice and quiet and writing a letter to his sister. But YOU know what he's thinking. HE'S thinking about waiting until you're asleep, sliding down your fatigues and DOING THINGS to you!

THAT is the problem with gay marriage. It's not the fact that it's same sex have sex with the same sex (as long as it's only women). It's not that anal sex is disgusting, because who hasn't tried to get away with it at least once in a heterosexual relationship (sorry, honey... I missed!) or that we find oral sex to be immoral and de facto sodomy (which we don't even when we say we do).

The bottom line (giggle) is that stupid straight people are scared that rampaging hoards of GAYS are going to ATTACK THEM and FORCE THEIR wing wangs up their pooter holes and OBAMA SAYS IT'S OK NOW!

THAT'S the problem!

I counted for you. 1,413 words. Out of which, 175 were loosely associated with a possibility of there being an anal rape, although the pretend person's pretend partner gave consent, then withdrew consent, and wasn't happy with how long it took him to withdraw himself after she withdrew consent. So, no rape.

And I was not "fired" from the Daily Kos. I was not paid by the Daily Kos. I did this for free. I was banned from DK because Markos Moulitsas seems to be allowing the inmates to run the asylum. I wasn't properly deferential to a group of professional victims who believed I should have ruined whatever satire was in the column by publishing "trigger warnings," like BE CAREFUL! THIS IS SATIRE ABOUT MEN PUTTING THEIR WALLY WALLIES IN GIRLS BUTT'S, WITH HER CONSENT AT FIRST, THEN SHE CHANGES HER MIND AND HE GETS OUT OF THERE, BUT NOT AS FAST AS SHE WOULD HAVE LIKED. THE WHOLE SEQUENCE IS A BIT MORE THAN 12% OF THE ENTIRE COLUMN.

But, the DK has lost a lot of good writers this way because Markos gives in to the little cults of personality and cliques that crop up, rather than trouble himself to actually run his own website.

Somehow, this is my fault.

And when I point out the FACT that the 175 words were NOT about rape but were about CLUMSINESS, that doesn't fit the Doctrine or the Canon, therefore it is deemed Apocryphal and not included in the official Dogma.

Get it?

8 THROW IN THE TOWEL?

I'm thinking that the author of "Trouble at the Koolaid Point" is throwing in the towel. I hope I am incorrect.

WHAT NEXT?

No idea. But I do think we need more options for online spaces, and I hope *one* of those spaces allows the kind of public conversations and learning we had on Twitter but where women — or anyone — does not feel an undercurrent of fear watching her follower count increase. Where there's no such thing as The Koolaid Point. And I also know the worst possible approach would be more aggressive banning, or restricting speech (especially not that), or restricting anonymity. I don't think Twitter needs to (or even can, at this point) do anything at all. I think *we* need to do something.

We can do this. I know we can. And many of you — especially you javaranchers — you know why I'm so certain. You've seen a million visitors a month in a male-dominated community year after year after year maintain a culture defined by a single TOS: *be nice*. You've seen how learning thrives in an environment where you can be fearless with questions and generous with answers. If millions of programmers can maintain one of the *largest* and most vibrant developer communities online*, for 15 years*, *without harassment of any kind*, then anyone can. Good luck trying to convince me it can't be done. Because I have something the trolls do not— *evidence*.

If you made it this far, I cannot possibly express how grateful I am for the wonderful experiences I had during the time I was on Twitter as [redacted]. The appreciation for the horses made my heart sing. And those of you who have ever talked with me there, or sent me pony pictures, or ever sent me a message or spoken to me at a conference about what you learned from me, you have done more for me than you will ever know.

And I miss you all right now. I miss hearing the stories about your life and your work and your thoughts and your pets, especially your pets. But again, it's not like I'm GONE gone.

After all, the ponies have only just begun to learn to code...

When I know where *they'll* be, you will be the first to know :) And when you all find a new space, that feels right, I know you will let me know.

<3, *[redacted]*

[footnote-I-wish-I-didn't-have-to-add: it's been brought to my attention that my complaints about weev's dox of me were apparently (and bizarrely) twisted to suggest I thought prostitution and being a victim of domestic violence were somehow "shameful." That THIS must be the reason I didn't want that narrative out there. First, that's, well, I don't even. Second, OMG you have no idea what I and my children have experienced in our lives so please, let go of the "Kathy hates that dox therefore Kathy hates prostitutes and victims of domestic violence. You know nothing of my life, so please stop imagining you know what I think, feel, or have been through. Quit trying to shoehorn me into a she-must-have-deserved-it-see-she-is-a-bad-person narrative. My reasons for not wanting a false backstory about my children to be publicized by a prominent troll has nothing at all to do with "shame" and everything to do with "actual truth". Because even if you believe *I* deserved to be doxxed, the story of my children was not weev's to tell (or let's say it was not up to the person-pretending-to-be-weev-that-weev-thinks-did-this-awesome-thing-to-me)]

It is tempting to think that I could just stop tweeting, stop blogging and these cretins would leave me alone. But it is daydreaming.

As I wrote earlier in the book, I tried that. They just got more and more annoying and obnoxious, sending death threats and warning via e-mail and blog comments and Twitter, and frankly I NEED Twitter to market my radio station my books, my audiobooks and other things I am selling in my ongoing effort to raise money for Parkinson's disease.

I tried ignoring them. So, they spammed the National Parkinson Foundation with what a hateful person I am and did they really want an anal rape enthusiast, a deranged cyberstalker, representing their brand? Ever courageous, the NPF asked me to remove their logo from my website (although they never did get around to returning my donations.)

When the Examiner agreed to take me back on using a pseudonym, these people spammed and trolled the editors at that website until they decided I just wasn't worth it any more and they cut me loose.

When Alan Colmes agreed to let me provide free columns for his Liberland blog, these people spammed him and spammed him and spammed him, but Alan ignored them. So they spammed the comment section for the stories I wrote and advised the liberal readers of Liberaland to "Google" my name to see what a horrid person I am, not realizing, apparently, that liberals would recognize that the only entries on Google that a bad word to say about me are right wing extremist hate sites.

So, why this level of "devotion" or "obsession?"
BECAUSE THEY'RE PSYCHOTIC!

9 YOU HEARD ME! PSYCHOTIC!

Roger Dooley is the author of Brainfluence: 100 Ways to Persuade and Convince Consumers with Neuromarketing. He has a piece about Internet trolls posted on the Oct. 6, 2014 online edition of Forbes.

The title?
INTERNET TROLLS REALLY ARE PSYCHOS

If you've ever managed an online community, a blog, or a brand's <u>*Facebook*</u> *page, you have encountered the dreaded "troll." These community members can be provocative and rude, and are known for creating posts for the sole purpose of agitating their fellow members. Trolls add inflammatory comments not because they hope to inform or convince others, but because they know they'll spark an avalanche of negativity.*

Left unchecked, trolls can destroy communities. Helpful members tire of the conflict and eventually leave. Trolls present a challenge to community managers not just because of their toxic behavior, but because they don't always overtly break community rules. Many people make comments that prove to be inflammatory, often unintentionally. Trollish behavior is evident only after a pattern of such comments emerges.

Conventional wisdom says that the anonymity of the Internet lets people behave in ways they never would in real life, or online if their identity was known. But, if you think that means that trolls are normally nice people who only act out in their online persona, think again. New research shows that internet trolls are, in real life, narcissists, psychopaths, and sadists.

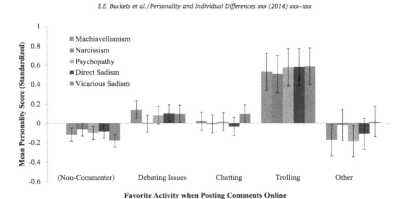

E.E. Buckels et al. / Personality and Individual Differences xxx (2014) xxx–xxx

Fig. 1. Dark Tetrad scores as a function of favorite online activity in Study 1. Error bars represent standard errors.

The paper's title, <u>Trolls Just Want To Have Fun</u>, is amusing, but the findings are anything but funny. Canadian researchers surveyed more than a thousand internet users about their commenting behavior. They then administered a personality test designed to measure, among other things, what's known as the Dark Tetrad. That's a measure of negative traits: sadism, psychopathy, narcissism, and Machiavellianism.

The correlation between these negative traits and trollish behavior was striking. No other kind of community participation showed such a relationship.

The research validates what most community managers have always believed: trolls are awful people in real life, too.

These results may not be of much use in curbing trolls online, but it does suggest that trying to stop the behavior by gentle coaching is doomed to fail most of the time. That, too, won't surprise experienced community operators. In my years of community building, I've seen a few trolls that actually tried to mend their ways but inevitably reverted to their old ways.

Since trolls actually derive pleasure from the suffering of others, engaging with them at all can be counter-productive. Instead, follow the simple maxim of experienced community leaders: "Don't feed the trolls."

Except, as the author of **Trouble at the Koolaid Point** and I have proven here, the Trolls Bring Their Own Lunch!

When this study was released, I got e-mails and Tweets from MY trolls saying, basically, "Look! Dey wrot a storee aboud youuu! Duhhhh."

They don't SEE themselves as trolls, by and large. In my case, they see themselves as holy crusaders, out to save the Internet from my evil doxing of dead babies and tormenting of grieving rape victims and other such nonsense that has been fabricated for their entertainment.

And those who DO see themselves as trolls – are PROUD of it.

The author of Trouble at the Koolaid Point refers to a troll called "weev." This twerp was the subject of a recent story by Natasha Lennard on the web site VICE NEWS. The title?

THE DANGER OF LETTING MONSTERS PASS AS INTERNET TROLLS.

When Brenda Leyland was asked by a reporter why she was sending abusive tweets to the parents of missing child Madeleine McCann, <u>she responded</u>: "I'm entitled to do that."

Whether she knew it or not, Leyland, who was found dead in a hotel room from a reported suicide on October 4, revealed a lot in that one comment. Accused of being among Twitter "trolls" who have written thousands of fiercely negative tweets about the McCanns, Leyland found refuge in a claim to entitlement. Whether she was in fact "entitled" to anonymously spew bile about the controversial parents is moot. She never faced legal consequences in life, and no sense of entitlement survives death.

Leyland was correct, though. To be granted the title "troll" is to be gifted a certain entitlement. Trolls enjoy the privilege of the benefit of moral doubt. Even the word suggests an impish nuisance or troublemaker, a bully at worst. But a number of recent incidents have shown darker monsters can hide behind troll masks.

Ms. Lennard does not pull her punches.

Nor does she spare herself from criticism.

It is a lesson myself and a number of fellow writers and journalists recently learned (or should have learned) the hard way in the case of Andrew "Weev" Auerheimer. Weev was unjustly imprisoned under the overreaching Computer Fraud and Abuse Act (CFAA) for exploiting a hole in iPad and AT&T security, then released on a legal technicality after a year in prison. He recently revealed himself to be a neo-Nazi, delineating his hatred of black and Jewish people and exposing a swastika chest tattoo on a white supremacist website. I shouldn't need to say that he is indefensible — not because the CFAA charges were just, but because he is a neo-Nazi.

Before Weev was a known neo-Nazi, he was called a "troll," and his online homophobia, anti-Semitism, and abuse was dismissed as "antics." I called him "tongue in cheek," and commended his "defiance" during his sentencing. The story of Weev is a parable about the dangers of letting ambiguity fog judgment when signs point all too clearly to putrid views. Which is neither to foreclose internet mischief and disruption, nor to insist on total online transparency.

Ethical hackers like Jeremy Hammond, serving 10 years in federal prison for his involvement in the LulzSec Stratfor hack, make abundantly clear that online rupture, aimed at seats of corporate power, needn't be the purview of bigots and misogynists. Trolls exempt themselves from appropriate censure with a sea of red herring arguments. Leyland's comment that she was "entitled" aligns with a tendency, primarily exhibited by white male trolls, to assert that their online activity is righteous simply because it has been permitted and is speech (and thus should be free).

She closes on a strong point.

Rather than wait for the criminal justice system or bottom-line-focused tech giants to do the work of stamping out online abuse, the ethical onus rests on individual online users to collectively refuse to countenance, engage, or be entertained by abusive discourse — and to call it when we see it. I shouldn't have waited for a man to display a swastika on his chest to recognize and decry his fascism.

The first thing that has to happen, companies like Facebook and Twitter and free blogging platforms like WordPress.com need to abide by their already-in-place Terms of Service.

10 LET'S ALL POINT AND LAUGH AT THE WORDPRESS.COM TERMS OF SERVICE

I have lost count of how many times I have reported the Thinking Man's Zombie blog, a WordPress.com blog, for violation of the WordPress.com terms of service.

Examples? OK.

Terms of Service:

Responsibility of Contributors. If you operate a blog, comment on a blog, post material to the Website, post links on the Website, or otherwise make (or allow any third party to make) material available by means of the Website (any such material, "Content"), You are entirely responsible for the content of, and any harm resulting from, that Content. That is the case regardless of whether the Content in question constitutes text, graphics, an audio file, or computer software.

By making Content available, you represent and warrant that:

> o the downloading, copying and use of the Content will not infringe the proprietary rights, including but not limited to the

copyright, patent, trademark or trade secret rights, of any third party;

- o if your employer has rights to intellectual property you create, you have either (i) received permission from your employer to post or make available the Content, including but not limited to any software, or (ii) secured from your employer a waiver as to all rights in or to the Content;
- o you have fully complied with any third-party licenses relating to the Content, and have done all things necessary to successfully pass through to end users any required terms;
- o the Content does not contain or install any viruses, worms, malware, Trojan horses or other harmful or destructive content;

- o the Content is not spam, is not machine- or randomly-generated, and does not contain unethical or unwanted commercial content designed to drive traffic to third party sites or boost the search engine rankings of third party sites, or to further unlawful acts (such as phishing) or mislead recipients as to the source of the material (such as spoofing);

In His Own Words

Posted: June 11, 2014 | Author: Paul Krendler | Filed under: Commentary, Discredit by quotation, Open Thread | 22 Comments

I didn't write this. Bill Schmalfeldt did. I took it from his blog to demonstrate his true self-image, the true nature of his character. And here's another example of Bill Schmalfeldt's own words, also taken from the same post:

"Therefore, their use qualifies as 'fair use' for the purpose of demonstration and criticism."

Ladies and Gentlemen, I present Bill Schmalfeldt's raging id:

So, my wife beats me, I crap my pants, I fabricate imaginary threats, because I'm a "screwed up individual." Oh yeah, and really really demented, too! I steal people's stuff. I write lies.

He said it, not me.

- o the Content is not pornographic, does not contain threats or incite violence, and does not violate the privacy or publicity rights of any third party;

- o your blog is not getting advertised via unwanted electronic messages such as spam links on newsgroups, email lists, other blogs and web sites, and similar unsolicited promotional methods;
- o your blog is not presented in a manner that misleads your readers into thinking that you are another person or company; and
- o you have, in the case of Content that includes computer code, accurately categorized and/or described the type, nature, uses and effects of the materials, whether requested to do so by Automattic or otherwise.

2. **Responsibility of Website Visitors.** Automattic has not reviewed, and cannot review, all of the material, including computer software, posted to the Website, and cannot therefore be responsible for that material's content, use or effects. By operating the Website, Automattic does not

represent or imply that it endorses the material there posted, or that it believes such material to be accurate, useful or non-harmful. You are responsible for taking precautions as necessary to protect yourself and your computer systems from viruses, worms, Trojan horses, and other harmful or destructive content. The Website may contain content that is offensive, indecent, or otherwise objectionable, as well as content containing technical inaccuracies, typographical mistakes, and other errors. The Website may also contain material that violates the privacy or publicity rights, or infringes the intellectual property and other proprietary rights, of third parties, or the downloading, copying or use of which is subject to additional terms and conditions, stated or unstated. Automattic disclaims any responsibility for any harm resulting from the use by visitors of the Website, or from any downloading by those visitors of content there posted.

3. **Content Posted on Other Websites.** We have not reviewed, and cannot review, all of the material, including computer software, made available through the websites and webpages to which WordPress.com links, and that link to WordPress.com. Automattic does not have any control over those non-WordPress websites and webpages, and is not responsible for their contents or their use. By linking to a non-WordPress website or webpage, Automattic does not represent or imply that it endorses such

website or webpage. You are responsible for taking precautions as necessary to protect yourself and your computer systems from viruses, worms, Trojan horses, and other harmful or destructive content. Automattic disclaims any responsibility for any harm resulting from your use of non-WordPress websites and webpages.

4. **Copyright Infringement and DMCA Policy.** As Automattic asks others to respect its intellectual property rights, it respects the intellectual property rights of others. If you believe that material located on or linked to by WordPress.com violates your copyright, you are encouraged to notify Automattic in accordance with Automattic's Digital Millennium Copyright Act ("DMCA") Policy. Automattic will respond to all such notices, including as required or

appropriate by removing the infringing material or disabling all links to the infringing material. Automattic will terminate a visitor's access to and use of the Website if, under appropriate circumstances, the visitor is determined to be a repeat infringer of the copyrights or other intellectual property rights of Automattic or others. In the case of such termination, Automattic will have no obligation to provide a refund of any amounts previously paid to Automattic.

5. **Intellectual Property.** This Agreement does not transfer from Automattic to you any Automattic or third party intellectual property, and all right, title and interest in and to such property will remain (as between the parties) solely with Automattic. Automattic, WordPress, WordPress.com, the WordPress.com logo, and all other trademarks, service marks, graphics and logos used in connection with WordPress.com, or the Website are trademarks or registered trademarks of Automattic or Automattic's licensors. Other trademarks, service marks, graphics and logos used in connection with the Website may be the trademarks of other third parties. Your use of the Website grants you no right or license to reproduce or otherwise use any Automattic or third-party trademarks.

My New Business Venture

Posted: July 29, 2014 | **Author:** Paul Krendler | **Filed under:** ELEVENTY, Fair Use, Humor, Parody, Transformative, What I've Been Up To | **Tags:** Fair Use, Humor, Parody, Shenanigans | 7 Comments

Since my current digs are so affordable (rent free, baby!) and spacious, and I have an absentee landlord (one might say he's ... wait for it... *out of his mind*), I thought I might start a little home business.

It's a niche restaurant. Craft beer and condiments.

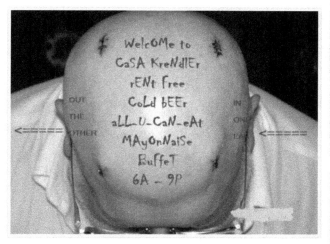

THIS

is what happens when someone challenges me. I have fun.

All I have – is *FUN!*

6. Etc. and Etc.

11. 293 COMMENTS ON ONE POST, ALL FILLED WITH HATE

The following comments, with my thoughts inserted, are all from one post on the Thinking Man's Zombie blog.

Dr_Mike — October 2, 2014 at 7:43 am

👍 4 👎 0 Rate This

Some people are like Slinkys, they make a lot of noise and serve no useful purpose, but man can they bring a smile to your face when you push them down a flight of stairs.

Reply — **Yeah, I know people like that.**

Howard D. Earl (@embryriddlealum) — October 2, 2014 at 9:13 am

👍 5 👎 1 Rate This

Some people are still alive but their whore mothers died while they blogged.

Reply — **A violation of the WordPress.com Terms of Service, but who's counting, right?**

Eddie Blake — October 2, 2014 at 9:50 am

👍 6 👎 0 Rate This

Some people are like dark clouds, so when they fuck off and die it's a brighter day.

Reply — **You got anybody in mind, Eddie?**

Howard D. Earl (@embryriddlealum)   October 2, 2014 at 10:46 am

👍 5 👎 0 ⓘ Rate This

I have the Sea Hag going first in the pool.

If for no other reason than the LULZ!

Chris Heather thinks my wife dying would be funny.

Reply

 Eddie Blake   October 2, 2014 at 12:08 pm

👍 3 👎 0 ⓘ Rate This

Some people have to kill their mothers to in order gain the intimate knowledge that they never had as child.

Speaking from experience, Eddie?

Reply

 EPWJ   October 2, 2014 at 11:25 am

👍 11 👎 2 ⓘ Rate This

Hey its not like wondering if ISIS would kidnap a guy and saw his head off, or mention that a woman lives at an address and needs to be gang raped…. or printing locations of children serving their country so terrorist no where to find them and rape them and kill them or threatening women with arrest deportation and separation from their children cause WALKER!

Its not like threatening to kill someone for writing about Brett Kimberlin, its not like threatening to beat a father of two in front of his wife and children because BRETT – its not like writing books about heart patients who are sued by Kimberlin and writing screeds about his wife and son and threatening to kill them too – its not like threatening a former US Attorney with a baseball bat

yeah – its not like that   **All things I've never done, Eric. But you know that, right? Just like you knew you were filing false reviews on Amazon, right?**

Reply

Gus Bailey   October 2, 2014 at 12:55 pm

👍 4 👎 0 ☆ Rate This

APOPHASIS!!!!

Reply   **Hey! Someone taught Gus one o' them $5 words!**

 Army Vet   October 2, 2014 at 12:29 pm

👍 5 👎 0 ☆ Rate This

Chris is Chris, and Jerry is Chris, and Howard is Chris. Now Bob Smallmind is Chris. How many
more people are Chris? Am I Chris? Is Paul Chris? Everyone is Chris.

Reply   **You're confused, Johnstown boy! Chris is Chris. He had a
dozen or so sock puppets. Do try to stay with the rest of
the class? There's a good lad.**

 Gus Bailey   October 2, 2014 at 12:57 pm

👍 4 👎 0 ☆ Rate This

I am Spart.... Chri... Ky... KRENNNDDDLLEEEERRRRRR

Reply   **There's Gus, adding value to the discussion.**

 Howard D. Earl (@embryriddlealum)   October 2, 2014 at 12:39 pm

👍 5 👎 0 ☆ Rate This   **That explains the rotting cheese smell.**

AND...POOF!!!

Reply

EPWJ   **October 2, 2014 at 12:41 pm**

👍 9 👎 4 ⓘ Rate This

balmer liberal cannot play
balmerliberal went away

Tweets of death and tweets of threats
violate the law, good taste and breath

The vileness of his screeds will be
his further undoing for all to see

For I am the Law the ACME man pled   **Eric don't need no**
Somewhere the law finally said   **steenking pentameter**

That enough is enough is enough you bad man
and now the the vile monster needs a new plan

His one saving grace is his mobile abode
easier for him when he flees on the road

Reply

Sarah   **October 2, 2014 at 12:56 pm**

👍 8 👎 0 ⓘ Rate This

"The crowd wildly applauds. But softly. Because this is a coffee house, dammit. And we
must be tasteful. And this was full of taste."

Reply   **They applaud nonsensical shit at coffee houses.**

Gus Bailey   **October 2, 2014 at 12:58 pm**

👍 4 👎 0 ⓘ Rate This   **We don't have tires. We have "tires."**
                                Welcome to America.
The tyres are dry rotted.

Reply

97

WILLIAM M. SCHMALFELDT, SR.

◻◻ *EPWJ*   October 2, 2014 at 1:15 pm

👍 5 👎 0 ⊘ Rate This

3 month expired mayo can seal most rot – most

**Emblematic of the lack of creativity of my band of trolls, the
constant reference to mayonnaise. The author of the blog once
mentioned "foot longs with mayo" to insinuate my having oral sex
with my dead twin brother. Simple concepts for simple folks.**

◻◻ *EPWJ*   October 2, 2014 at 12:42 pm

👍 5 👎 1 ⊘ Rate This

He has no idea no idea that if he keeps poking……. in his next letter Johns judgments are not the
only disclaimers he's going to have to list

This makes no sense whatsoever.

Reply

> 🖼 *Howard D. Earl (@embryriddlealum)*   October 2, 2014 at 12:56 pm
>
> 👍 8 👎 0 ⊘ Rate This
>
> **I'd rather you weren't on my
> planet, Chris.**
>
> I believe I no longer want him on my Twitter.
>
> **Scat!**
>
> He has worn out his welcome.
>
> Reply
>
> > ◻◻ *EPWJ*   October 2, 2014 at 1:16 pm
> >
> > **Eric is vying for the title of most
> > prolific hate troll.**
> >
> > 👍 7 👎 0 ⊘ Rate This
> >
> > 2.6 years ago……….

Eddie Blake   October 2, 2014 at 1:02 pm

👍 5 👎 0 ⚙ Rate This

(Don't Contact Me + X!) = Twitter suspension for some people.

Reply   **We all know that the "stop contacting me" rule only works for conservatives.**

> *EPWJ*   October 2, 2014 at 1:14 pm
>
> 👍 7 👎 1 ⚙ Rate This
>
> He doesn't realize that Twitter is a private company and if you are banned you are not allowed to return and can be actually breaking the law in some areas by repeatedly trying to access – ask Debra Frisch how that turned out for her -
>
> Reply   **But it's OK when @embryriddlealum and @alumembryriddle and all his various sock puppets do it. And yes, the jails are FULL of Twitter TOS violators.**

🔅 *Techno Jinxx*   October 2, 2014 at 1:21 pm

👍 7 👎 0 ⚙ Rate This

DAMN, that was fast, you'd think eventually he'd learn to just leave people alone after his 5th or 6th suspension, but NOOOoooooOOOOOo, not Shakey, he just keeps on trying bless his rotten little heart.

Reply   **I complained about someone contacting me when I told him to stop. Twitter took quick and decisive action and suspended me. Problem solved.**

> *EPWJ*   October 2, 2014 at 1:32 pm
>
> 👍 6 👎 3 ⚙ Rate This
>
> I just got spoofed —- calling police now
>
> Reply   **I think you mean "swatted," right bunkie? Cops don't care if someone "spoofs" you.**

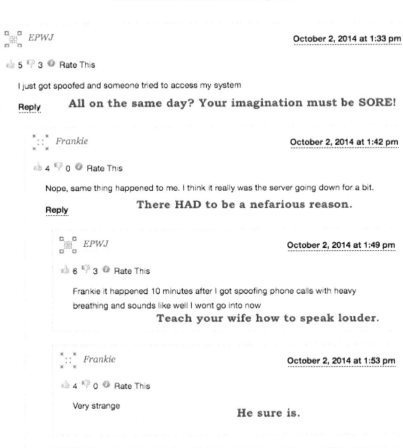

EPWJ   October 2, 2014 at 1:33 pm

5 3 Rate This

I just got spoofed and someone tried to access my system

Reply   **All on the same day? Your imagination must be SORE!**

Frankie   October 2, 2014 at 1:42 pm

4 0 Rate This

Nope, same thing happened to me. I think it really was the server going down for a bit.

Reply   **There HAD to be a nefarious reason.**

EPWJ   October 2, 2014 at 1:49 pm

6 3 Rate This

Frankie it happened 10 minutes after I got spoofing phone calls with heavy
breathing and sounds like well I wont go into now

Teach your wife how to speak louder.

Frankie   October 2, 2014 at 1:53 pm

4 0 Rate This

Very strange

He sure is.

nottherealbill   October 2, 2014 at 1:53 pm

4 0 Rate This

Was it a Mayo-y sound?

Ask your Mama.

Army Vet   **October 2, 2014 at 1:39 pm**

👍 7 👎 0 ⊘ Rate This

It's rather amusing at times. He gets banned, comes back and screeches at people to not contact him from an account he isn't supposed to have because he was banned in the first place. Schmalfail logic on display.

Reply   **It's also amusing how Army boy here knows my every move, my every tweet, and has a file cabinet filled with my every written word.**

 *nottherealbill*   **October 2, 2014 at 1:43 pm**

👍 4 👎 0 ⊘ Rate This

he tried a post on this one **https://twitter.com/Injusticebuster/with_replies** but got called out and deleted it   **Nope. Wrong.**

Reply

> *Frankie*   **October 2, 2014 at 1:56 pm**
>
> 👍 6 👎 0 ⊘ Rate This
>
> looks like he is reviving any old account he can remember. Damn he had a lot of accounts.   **If you say so, Frankie.**
>
> **Reply**
>
> > *Techno Jinxx*   **October 2, 2014 at 2:58 pm**
> >
> > 👍 5 👎 0 ⊘ Rate This
> >
> > doesn't Twitter's TOS say something about multiple accounts???
> > **Ask Chris Heather about that.**

Kyle Kiernan   October 2, 2014 at 3:54 pm

👍 9 👎 0 ⚙ Rate This

is this like the end of Terminator 2 where the shape shifter Terminator is dying in
the metal vat and cycles through all his past identities?

Neat.

Gotta go. Gotta get back to my D&D or maybe I gotta do crimes. Maybe I gotta
do crimes in LARP mode. I never can tell what persona I'm supposed to be at
any one moment. **Take a PRETTY mug shot next time.**

A Reader #1   October 2, 2014 at 6:30 pm

👍 5 👎 0 ⚙ Rate This   **If you need to know where I am and what**
                          I'm doing at any particular time, the
It;s back again.   **Tapeworm here is the boy to ask.**

Reply

A Reader #1   October 2, 2014 at 1:58 pm

👍 8 👎 0 ⚙ Rate This

This is just crazy. Patrick Grady, Chris Heather, and EPWJ are all Ahab's current white whales.
Heavy breathing on calls and who knows what else? I suggesevade targets be on guard for
SWATing, too. By the way, if my "beloved" had injured herself and needed to use a cane, I would
not be spending my time creating vulgar hate blogs and tweeting threats and profanities.

Reply   **What am I supposed to be doing? Hovering over her?**
        Staring at her, waiting for her to explode? Dimwit.

Techno Jinxx   October 2, 2014 at 2:55 pm

👍 8 👎 0 ⚙ Rate This

well yeah, because I'm sure you actually care about your "beloved", can't make the same
assumption about Shakey. His actions over the last few days pretty much shows he
doesn't.   **Can't say how, exactly, but saying it makes it**
Reply   **true! It is now in the Doctrine and Canon!**

A Reader #1   October 2, 2014 at 6:08 pm

👍 4 👎 0 Rate This

Over at his latest PD advocacy site, * cough, cough, cough* I mean vulgar and homoerotic blog, he is making fun of EPWJ and, apparently, me – seems I struck a nerve when I commented about the time he is wasting tipping at windmills instead of caring for the person he calls his "beloved" and his "bride." Uh, huh.

Reply   **Once again, the simplicity of the Lickspittle Troll is demonstrated. I said I wanted to concentrate more on PD advocacy. Therefore everything I do MUST be PD related.**

> *A Reader #1*   October 2, 2014 at 6:09 pm
>
> 👍 5 👎 0 Rate This
>
> Oh, I forgot to mention that he seems obsessed with Grady's penis and his own mother's . . . "po po." I get that impression from the header on the blog plus blog entries entitled "The Truth About Grady's Penis."
>
> Reply   **As if the Tapeworm was anyone to talk about being "obsessed" by someone.**

Paul Krendler   October 2, 2014 at 6:14 pm

👍 8 👎 6 Rate This

It's important to remember that the weapons he uses to attack people are not the ones that hurt them the most...they are the ones that hurt *HIM* the most.

Just something to keep in mind.   **Is that the purpose of your blog, Paul? To HURT me? Why do you want to do THAT? What did I do to you?**

Reply

> **Howard D. Earl (@embryriddlealum)**   October 2, 2014 at 7:42 pm
>
> 👍 4 👎 0 Rate This
>
> Exactly.   **Shut up, Chrissy.**
>
> Reply

Rain   October 2, 2014 at 6:35 pm

👍 6 👎 0 ⊘ Rate This

Damn, looks like I missed all the fun again.

It's always sad to see someone so filled with hate, that all they can do with their time is spew it everywhere instead of trying to do something good with their lives...

But oh well, Little Bitch spewing hate will always be a whining little bitch spewing hate, cause that's all he can be apparently.

O.o   **Every time this failed songwriter posts something, it is almost exactly the same.**

Reply

Howard D. Earl (@embryriddlealum)   October 2, 2014 at 7:42 pm

👍 8 👎 0 ⊘ Rate This

"The Free Speech Warriors got BalmerLiberal taken down, and all i did was complain about being harassed. "

Sorry, gas bag. You don't get a free slate with every new account.

Reply   **But YOU will get three hots and a cot, Chrissy!**

EPWJ

October 3, 2014 at 8:36 am

👍 7 👎 8 🔄 Rate This

5 years online and five friends on facebook and all he can do is to watch the further research done to his actions

oooooh he's soooo powerful its Friday and strangely the reviews are still going strong thanks to his exposure

Did you know that his dopamine book is nothing more than a hate hit against family members and conservatives? Wow its not about coping with a horrible disease – its about his very needy need to need to hate.

Color me surprised –

oh will have some passages the use of profanity – the cursing of family members – the endless affection (affliction) of these tome's to humanity garnished spicely with the n word

Reply

Eric is putting together a dossier of things that are not against the law, plus things I have not done.

EPWJ

October 3, 2014 at 8:40 am

👍 6 👎 6 🔄 Rate This

the family picture, I have not ever criticized his family especially like he does – but sometimes stuff could be left out of books – for their sake

Also as he sits their quivering with the molten rage of a thousand cowards words, keep on reporting yourself to law enforcement – strangely – except for you calling me yesterday – no one gives a hoot –

Reply

"THE MOLTEN RAGE OF A THOUSAND COWARDS!"
That's a LOT of molten rage.
Does laughing at you count?

EPWJ

October 3, 2014 at 8:44 am

👍 6 👎 4 🔄 Rate This

hey stuff guy – I am sending to all concerned parties your own recording of your harassing a rape victims health fundraiser last year – the attacks on her family – etc – I am also adding it to the legal papers being filed and to spread the word about the man who attacks rape victims

WHAT rape victim?

you mocked that she needed the money to go to CPAC, nice

EPWJ   October 3, 2014 at 9:06 am

👍 7 👎 11 ⊘ Rate This

Twitter can get several thousand dollars per instant of trespass – I didn't know that – also – deliberate actions like that can carry non-concurrent sentencing of several months – each – I didn't know that – I think – that 50/60/75 twitter handles obtained after being banned – could in almost every known court in the land constitute stalking

I didn't know this maybe that's why some of these legal departments are actually calling now, mailing postage paid envelopes to send material in – instead of sending links

And haven't even sent them anything yet

I wonder how the FTc, the FBI, and all those LEO's would think of the 1,739 pieces of evidence gathered so far – the firings – the bannings – the death threats – the porn – the hate crimes – the fraud of pretending to raise money – and the crimes against basic character development and sentence structure –

False reporting I heard in my county carries a mandatory sentence of 11 months and 29 days – the reason for that sentence is that hypothetically any moron with 50/60/75 identities who fails to disclose that he is harassing grieveing widows, rape victims, single mothers, parents of challenged children who sends them an obviously fake letter to complain about harassment to further harass – well any idiot who would be sooo freakin stupid to piss off a rural hanging judge or two, will be a guest of the county and no, they won't be spending their days at taxpayer expense – they would be sentenced to PROBATION.

If any idiot moron had thought ahead, he would know that PROBATION has to be served in this county.

Most good Christian people around here like their military girls like those who were honored to be nominated to the academies and probably are not going to bend over to accommodate extra refrigeration for mayo. Good luck finding rental space, if someone was stupid enough to complain and make up false charges while conducting crimes all over the internet.

we are quivering in fear........ ahahahahahahahahahahahaha

Reply   **Each post more disjointed than the one before.**

librarygryffon

👍 5 👎 0 ⊘ Rate This

I note he's been really, *really* quiet the last 24 hours....

Does an instance of trespass mean each account acquired after being banned, or each tweet? Thought even if the former, those fines are adding up fast.

TN requires most probationers to pay a monthly fee (admittedly modest) to help cover expenses of supervision and victim restitution. And I wouldn't imagine that they'd jump at the idea of transferring someone to MD's care for probation given how little concern MD has shown about the behaviour up to now.

Reply

Actually, I was working on an audiobook. But I like your fears of a nefarious purpose better.

EPWJ

October 3, 2014 at 12:19 pm

👍 5 👎 10 ⊘ Rate This

naw he's creating facebook stuff and building websites, but no one but LEO's are going to see...

Have you had a stroke recently, Eric?

EPWJ   October 3, 2014 at 12:15 pm

👍 7 👎 11 ⊘ Rate This

Tennessee has jurisdiction – because he sent a letter to Tennessee or pretended to send a letter to Tennessee – I haven't and won't do anything – I don't need to – I will assist them with 1,739 pieces of evidence – what I think the new DA is really going to go over the edge about, is the 91 minute tape where he broadcasts his total hate towards Mandy for her illness especially now that she is so very ill, and his gleeful doxing of her family, her finances, her liens and other things – he must have forgotten that the people who doxed joe the plumber – went quietly to jail (probation) and lost their govt jobs.

Things like that – I warned him MANY MANY MANY times that yes normally people will not give a hoot but once you piss off law enforcement – you are not going to like the consequences – sending that broadcast letter got me ZERO phone calls – why because they were already monitoring him, they already KNEW about him. His saving grace if it was all a bluff isn't going to help him either, because he posted it in an attempt to coerce me which didn't work.

Looking at depth of another book today that several pages were taken without permission and had nothing to do with coping with Parkinson's they were about self promotion, hate for some family members and screeds against conservatives.

Reply

Your life would be empty
without me, Eric!

⊞ *Rick Buchanan*   October 3, 2014 at 2:48 pm

👍 5 👎 1 ⊘ Rate This

I think any comprehensive listing of Bill's misdeeds just HAS to include this.

He lives near Baltimore, and when entertaining visitors from out of state, took them for a crab dinner — to JOE'S CRAB SHACK!

This is like a Maine resident taking people to Red Lobster!

Or a Brooklynite going to Domino's for pizza!

Or a Phily person getting cheese steak sandwiches from SUBWAY!

It ought to be categorized as a crime against humanity.

Reply   **Such is the extent of the trolling and stalking, they
comment on where we took our nephew to lunch.**

agiledog   **October 3, 2014 at 2:57 pm**

👍 3 👎 0 ⊘ Rate This

What? Red Lobster ISN'T a fine seafood place?

Crushed. I'm just crushed. (/sarc, just in case someone misses it)

If you are ever in central Mass., look for a place in Worcester called "The Sole Proprietor" – now that is a good seafood place.

Reply # Everyone LOVES Jane's cheesy biscuits!

     nottherealbill   **October 4, 2014 at 8:40 am**

     👍 0 👎 0 ⊘ Rate This

     Sole is OK but legal is better

EPWJ   **October 3, 2014 at 4:46 pm**

👍 4 👎 2 ⊘ Rate This

its the cheesy biscuits –

Reply

     Jane   **October 3, 2014 at 5:00 pm**

     👍 3 👎 0 ⊘ Rate This

     I make those at home so I don't have to go to Red Lobster to get them. 😊

Howard D. Earl (@embryriddlealum)   October 3, 2014 at 6:07 pm

👍 3 👎 1 ⚙ Rate This

That would be like taking someone to Taco Bell for real Mexican food here in The Valley.

Joe's makes that special mayonnaise.

Just saying.   **Another funny mayo reference.**

Reply

 EPWJ   October 3, 2014 at 5:28 pm

👍 7 👎 11 ⚙ Rate This

I'm guessing it was a stroke, right Eric? Or
Hey hey impotent man   **a tumor? Do you have a brain tumor?**
sitting all alone in his tin can

No one can hear you
no one can see

Your latest little efforts
to make me fear pee

But your urine again will flow down the deck
for as you dig deeper its your life you'll wreck

Reply

 EPWJ   October 3, 2014 at 5:36 pm

👍 6 👎 10 ⚙ Rate This   **Low and lazy.**

Hi Bill – how's it hangin?

Reply

Howard D. Earl (@embryriddlealum)   **October 3, 2014 at 8:54 pm**

👍 4 👎 3 ⊘ Rate This

He keeps this up, I may not be so gracious and continue allowing him to occupy my Twitter.

Reply

> *EPWJ*   **October 3, 2014 at 9:08 pm**
>
> 👍 4 👎 5 ⊘ Rate This
>
> Hi Bill! Since you are here – why did you spend time in your Parky books to spread hate?
>
> Curious

 EPWJ   **October 3, 2014 at 7:17 pm**

👍 7 👎 8 ⊘ Rate This

whats that Bill? I can't hear what you're saying?

Reply

> 🖼️ *Rain*   **October 3, 2014 at 9:19 pm**
>
> 👍 5 👎 0 ⊘ Rate This
>
> you know, it's not nice to tease a retard..
> Funny as all get out…
> but not nice…
>
> then again, Little Bitch generally asks for it daily so why not give it to him right?
>
> O.o
>
> **Reply**

Kimmy enjoys taunting the disabled.

EPWJ   **October 3, 2014 at 9:54 pm**

👍 4 👎 1 ⓘ Rate This

yeah makes a cartoon about my kid points to it on his new twitter feed – too late University police got screen grabs – of the tweets and the site –

now he goes dark soon to go blank…

Who made a cartoon about your kid? And why would it be illegal and something for the University Police?

 Howard D. Earl (@embryriddlealum)   **October 3, 2014 at 10:53 pm**

👍 4 👎 1 ⓘ Rate This

He protects his TL.

WIN! **Take your victories, however small, where you can find them, Chrissy.**

🖼 *Army Vet*   **October 4, 2014 at 8:56 am**

👍 5 👎 0 ⓘ Rate This

Notice he says he will only focus on PD. Notice that almost every post after that is vile lies and attacks on people that are not even speaking to him. Notice he has lied yet again. Shocking I know.

No, I did NOT say I would "only" focus on PD. You're making that up, doof!

Reply

🖼 *Howard D. Earl (@embryriddlealum)*   **October 4, 2014 at 9:42 am**

👍 4 👎 7 ⓘ Rate This

Time for the Sea Hag to take another "fall."

Reply **Who here filed a restraining order against a woman. Oh yeah, you! That was funny!**

EPWJ   **October 4, 2014 at 9:48 am**

👍 4 👎 6 ⊘ Rate This

Army vet – yeah using his website which he is clearly NOT raising funds – using the tweets to promote a Website where he is posting pictures of young girls

Hmmmmmmmm   **A wonderful, MAGICAL website that only Eric can see!**

Reply

     EPWJ   **October 4, 2014 at 10:12 am**

     👍 4 👎 7 ⊘ Rate This

     Yeah I can see the next letter to LAw enforcement

     So I wrote you last week but this week after I was banned twice in one day by twitter . Meanwhile today, when I broke into the service again, the father of some kid I keep posting her picture = he said mean things about me when I posted pictures of even more young girls that I didn't have permission to. look I had to spend hours lifting those pictures from copyrighted sources create the cartoons, and the build a website and post them because – I'm a fund raiser for PArkinsons – I mean one day I'll get around to it, its been 11 years but I'm optimistic!

     Arrest him immediately because I physically don't have the strength to spend 14 hours a day creating these site so people will be harmed…

     Where is MY pursuit of happiness, huh, MR law enforcement officers

     Signed

     Mr Certified Serial Adjudicated Harasser

     Certified? By who? You? A senile doof?

EPWJ   **October 4, 2014 at 10:17 am**

👍 3 👎 5 ⊘ Rate This

Just so you know I tried to capture the poor sentence structure and other grammatical missives of his spicy grimy gritty style.   **Your writing stands on it own stumps.**

Techno Jinxx

Look again, dimwit!

October 4, 2014 at 10:27 am

👍 3 👎 0 ⊘ Rate This

he says this over an hour ago

 WMS-DB
@WmsDb

🐦 Follow

Now, as a token of my sincere desire to end the silliness, I will take down my non-radio, non-book, non-Parkinson's advocacy websites.

9:📃 AM - 4 Oct 2014

↩ ⇄ ★

yet his nasty attacks he calls "satire" are still up at his cesspool blog.

hmmnn, could lead one to think he isn't serious.

Reply

jem

October 4, 2014 at 10:44 am

👍 3 👎 1 ⊘ Rate This

1. Abuse twitter
2. Post bad stuff on website.
3. Use twitter to offer bad website material as ransom.
4. Claim victimhood if not accepted.

Rinse, lather, ...

Did you get all that done in one day, or did it take awhile?

Reply

Howard D. Earl (@embryriddlealum)　　　　October 4, 2014 at 10:40 am

👍 4 👎 5 ⓘ Rate This

You poor dumb bastard (literally), Shakey. You are too dumb and far too obtuse to ever realize that you have never posted a pic that has anything to do with me. You have no idea who I am. You have never even been close.

You will know who I am on your death bed. I will make sure of it. And hopefully it will be soon.

Said the man married to his own Mommy! Nice death
Reply　　　**threat, though. I know the cops won't do anything, but**
still.... nice veiled threat there.

 Howard D. Earl (@embryriddlealum)　　　　October 4, 2014 at 10:45 am

👍 3 👎 6 ⓘ Rate This

I will take it upon myself now, to post the most vile photos, of every one of Bill Schmalfeldt's family members.
Did your mom ever blow a donkey?
Did your dad service Muslim prisoners?
Does Gail work Balmer street corners?
Photographic proof coming soon. Because I know who THEY are.

Be looking for my new wordpress site.

But by all means, keep doing what you're doing.

Reply　　**My Mommy died, so I can't marry her. How does that**
work, by the way? I know your daddy cakked in 2010,
but your MOM? Really?

 | Marriage Records

Name	Spouse	Location	Date	Date Reported
👤 Christopher S Heather	👤 Joanne Jean Heather	📍 Racine, WI	📅 N/A	📅 Jun 2012

EPWJ   October 4, 2014 at 11:23 am

👍 4 👎 6 ⊘ Rate This

Contacting Live365

Here are their TOS

. Content Guidelines/Prohibited Uses

a. Content Guidelines.

You agree not to post, upload or transmit to the Site or to Live365's servers any sound
recordings, communications, text, graphics, digital content, or other information (collectively,
"Material") that:

a.is obscene, fraudulent, indecent, discourteous, racially offensive, or abusive;

b.defames, abuses, harasses or threatens others;

c.contains any computer viruses, Trojan horses, worms, time bombs, cancelbots, ransomware,
rootkits, keyloggers, dialers, spyware, adware, malicious BHOs, rogue security software or other
malicious programs, disabling devices or other harmful component intended to damage,
detrimentally interfere with, surreptitiously intercept or expropriate any system, data or personal
information;

d.advocates or encourages any illegal activity;

e.infringes upon the copyright, patent, trademark, trade secret, publicity right or other intellectual
property or proprietary right of any third party;

f.violates the privacy of individuals, including other users of the Site; or

g.violates any applicable local, state, national, or international law.

Live365 in its sole discretion shall determine your compliance with the foregoing guidelines.
Live365 reserves the exclusive rights to delete from the Site without prior notice any material that
it deems to be non-complying or otherwise objectionable for any reason and to terminate,
suspend, and/or otherwise deny Site access to any user determined to have violated the
foregoing guidelines for any reason.   **I had to tell Eric I don't broadcast with
Live365.**

wonder how they are going to

Reply

EPWJ

October 4, 2014 at 2:28 pm

👍 4 👎 1 🔄 Rate This

Soundcloud TOS

(viii) You must not use the Platform to upload, post, store, transmit, display, copy, distribute, promote, make available or otherwise communicate to the public:

##any Content that is offensive, abusive, libellous, defamatory, obscene, racist, sexually explicit, ethnically or culturally offensive, indecent, that promotes violence, terrorism, or illegal acts, incites hatred on grounds of race, gender, religion or sexual orientation, or is otherwise objectionable in SoundCloud's reasonable discretion;

##any information, Content or other material that violates, plagiarises, misappropriates or infringes the rights of third parties including, without limitation, copyright, trademark rights, rights of privacy or publicity, confidential information or any other right; or

##any Content that violates, breaches or is contrary to any law, rule, regulation, court order or is otherwise is illegal or unlawful in SoundCloud's reasonable opinion;

##any material of any kind that contains any virus, Trojan horse, spyware, adware, malware, bot, time bomb, worm, or other harmful or malicious component, which or might overburden, impair or disrupt the Platform or servers or networks forming part of, or connected to, the Platform, or which does or might restrict or inhibit any other user's use and enjoyment of the Platform; or

##any unsolicited or unauthorised advertising, promotional messages, spam or any other form of solicitation.

(ix) You must not commit or engage in, or encourage, induce, solicit or promote, any conduct that would constitute a criminal offence, give rise to civil liability or otherwise violate any law or regulation.

Legal email sending now

The same sort of DEVOTED stalking that led Eric to write those false, negative reviews on Amazon! Bravo, Eric!

Reply

EPWJ   October 4, 2014 at 2:41 pm

👍 2 👎 1 ⊘ Rate This

Streamlicensing TOS

14. Our monitoring activity goes beyond ensuring compliance with Sections 112 and 114 of the Copyright Act. Therefore, your further agree to refrain from posting content: •That advocates or encourages illegal activity;

•That impersonates any person or entity or acts on behalf of another person or entity without authorization, including, but not limited to, a StreamLicensing™ employee or falsely states or otherwise misrepresents your affiliation with a person or entity;

•That includes personal or identifying information about another person without that person's explicit consent;

•That is false, deceptive, misleading, deceitful, misinformative, fraudulent, relates to hate-groups or other racist activities, or constitutes "bait and switch";

•That constitutes or contains any form of junk mail, spam, chain letter, pyramid scheme or other unsolicited or illegal commercial advertisement;

•That advertises any illegal service or the sale of any items the sale of which is prohibited or restricted by any applicable law, including without limitation items the sale of which is prohibited by law;

•That employs any tool to disguise the origin of content, including false or misleading E-mail addresses.

Legal email with detailed harassment screen caps being sent now

Reply   **This is the company that covers my music licensing.
             Again, a swing and a miss. But good stalking!**

EPWJ   October 4, 2014 at 3:03 pm

👍 2 👎 0 ⊘ Rate This

Like Brett someone's trying to use his kid as a human shield as the forces of good close in on his nefarious activities, running out of room to "raise" funds for Parkinsons?

Reply   **A little early in the day to be "sundowning" isn't it, Eric?**

Howard D. Earl (@embryriddlealum)   **October 4, 2014 at 3:46 pm**

👍 3 👎 0 ⚙ Rate This

"I guess we're gonna find out real soon if I'm right about Christopher S. Heather being @embryriddlealum. Now that the cops are involved…"

That schtick is as played out as your mother's pussy was, Shakey.

Reply   # Classy Boy!

 Perry Mason   **October 4, 2014 at 3:53 pm**

👍 2 👎 0 ⚙ Rate This

Really? You have to go there?

Reply   # It's all he's got!

 Howard D. Earl (@embryriddlealum)   **October 4, 2014 at 4:12 pm**

👍 1 👎 0 ⚙ Rate This

Yes. You ain't seen nothing yet.

You are a bore, Shakey. There was no death threat from me.

You've contacted no law enforcement. You don't have the balls.

Go ahead, Shake and Flake. I dare you.

And more to come!

CLASSY GROWN-UPS!

t

119

Perry Mason   **October 4, 2014 at 4:19 pm**

👍 3 👎 0 ⊘ Rate This

WMS-DB @WmsDb · 12m 12 minutes ago
Yes. He does, Perry. Desperate people do desperate things. The death threat was over the top.

There was no "death threat" you stinking POS.

Go crawl in a fucking hole.

I don't agree with ERA, but you deserve everything you get. And more.

Reply   # But, why?

> *Howard D. Earl (@embryriddlealum)*   **October 4, 2014 at 4:26 pm**
>
> 👍 3 👎 0 ⊘ Rate This
>
> Here's the thing, Shakey. They will tell you that I am not Chris H.
>
> They won't tell you who I am.
>
> And unlike you. I'm sure they can read. No death threat. Although with just a minimum of contact with you, they too will wish you would blow your brains out.
>
> And my only presence on Twitter is @embryriddlealum.
>
> You don't scare me, Jiggle.
>
> WORK ON IT!!
>
> **Reply**   # You're not smart enough to scare, Chrissy!

> *Howard D. Earl (@embryriddlealum)*   **October 4, 2014 at 5:40 pm**
>
> 👍 2 👎 0 ⊘ Rate This
>
> There will be no cop(s).
>
> I know that will make you crazy(ier), Seaman Slurper.
>
> I like that. A lot.   # Stand by! And WAIT!
>
> **Reply**

Howard D. Earl (@embryriddlealum)   **October 4, 2014 at 5:48 pm**

👍 2 👎 0 🔄 Rate This

Staying right where I am, Shakey. Which of course, isn't Wisconsin.

There will just be no police at my door.

I know that bugs you.   **Oh, right. That's because you are not you, not because you're going to take it on the lam or anything.**

Take THE CURE, Shakey!

 Howard D. Earl (@embryriddlealum)   **October 4, 2014 at 4:29 pm**

👍 3 👎 0 🔄 Rate This

That WAS fast, Shakey. Usually they take a bit longer to brush you off. String you out a little longer.   **Promising to investigate is a brush off?**

They must be watching the UW game.

I wonder if they were laughing when they pressed send.   **OK...**

Reply

 Howard D. Earl (@embryriddlealum)   **October 4, 2014 at 4:32 pm**

👍 4 👎 0 🔄 Rate This   **Just keep waiting, Chrissy.**

Make no mistake, Commodore Cuckolded.

That was a brush off.

I'm not laughing with you, SchmalScwanz. I'm laughing AT YOU.

Reply

librarygryffon **October 4, 2014 at 4:59 pm**

👍 6 👎 0 ⊘ Rate This

On the extremely off chance that the Elkridge PD takes him seriously and contacts WI, they would then prove that Heather is NOT Earl, and wouldn't that leave our boy Bill open to just tons and tons of harassment and libel charges not to mention filing false reports?

This would seem a rather dangerous step for someone to take who is so routinely wrong. Amusing as heck for the rest of us though. **Not Elkridge Police, honey. Maryland State Police.**

 Techno Jinxx **October 4, 2014 at 5:04 pm**

👍 4 👎 0 ⊘ Rate This

OH dear, I don't think Shakey thought this thru, IF Howard isn't Heather, I hope the police will take care of protecting him from the deranged cyber stalker who is obviously obsessed with him.

I also hope Shakey gets nailed for filing a false police report on the wrong person. **Right. 293 comments, and I'm the obsessed one.**

 Howard D. Earl (@embryriddlealum) **October 4, 2014 at 5:08 pm**

👍 4 👎 1 ⊘ Rate This

I will wait for a knock on the door that will never, ever come, Shakey.

You know it. **Keep waiting until I tell you differently.**

I know it.

We ALL know it.

librarygruffon   **October 4, 2014 at 6:04 pm**

👍 4 👎 0 ⊙ Rate This

He's got a great list of all the doxes he claims he got right. We *know* he's got Chris Heather and Kyle Kiernan wrong. And he's doxed at least two people as Tom Blvd, so at least one (if not both) of them are wrong. His doxing of Kimbery Dykes is doubtful, as well as Lynn Thomas (they keep linking to some poor librarian). Having discredited over half of his "I got it right!" doxes (and I'm sure there are more that he's not listing that were woefully wrong), I wouldn't think he'd really think that a record to be proud of.

Not to forget that poor woman in Oregon he claimed was P Mason. Bill seems to be trying to pretend that never happened.

You're getting repetitive, Nancy.

 jem   **October 4, 2014 at 6:10 pm**

👍 2 👎 0 ⊙ Rate This

Just recently, under his previous handle, he said he'd only missed ONE dox. Now admitting two. Keep doubling that a few times and he will soon be near the mark.

Keeping track? That's nice.

 Howard D. Earl (@embryriddlealum)   **October 4, 2014 at 6:13 pm**

👍 2 👎 1 ⊙ Rate This

He is here merely for my entertainment. When he assumes room temperature, he will be missed.

When you gonna grow a sack and TCOB, Chrissy?

Howard D. Earl (@embryriddlealum) — October 4, 2014 at 4:51 pm

👍 6 👎 1 ⊘ Rate This

You are dismissed, Shakey.

Reply

You are screwed, Chrissy.

 Howard D. Earl (@embryriddlealum) — October 4, 2014 at 5:45 pm

👍 5 👎 1 ⊘ Rate This

You really have no choice in the matter, Shakey.

I will continue to do as I please and you will just have to deal with it.

There is always THE CURE.

You can run away with the circus and find employment as an elephant's vibrator.

Reply

But you promised me a death bed visit!!!

 Howard D. Earl (@embryriddlealum) — October 4, 2014 at 5:50 pm

👍 2 👎 1 ⊘ Rate This

I am soliciting suggestions for my new wordpress page that is dedicated to photoshops of the dearly departed Schmalfedlts.

Reply

Still waiting for that, too!

Howard D. Earl (@embryriddlealum) — October 4, 2014 at 6:03 pm

👍 3 👎 2 ⊘ Rate This

Side note: ancestry.com doesn't really care if you are a member of the family you wish to research.

Reply

Just spell the name right.

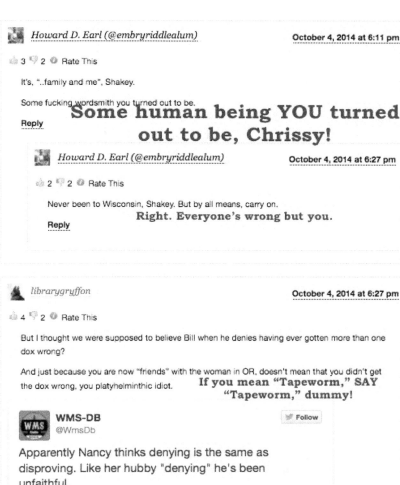

Howard D. Earl (@embryriddlealum) October 4, 2014 at 6:11 pm

👍 3 👎 2 ⊘ Rate This

It's, "..family and me", Shakey.

Some fucking wordsmith you turned out to be.

Some human being YOU turned out to be, Chrissy!

Reply

Howard D. Earl (@embryriddlealum) October 4, 2014 at 6:27 pm

👍 2 👎 2 ⊘ Rate This

Never been to Wisconsin, Shakey. But by all means, carry on.

Right. Everyone's wrong but you.

Reply

librarygryffon October 4, 2014 at 6:27 pm

👍 4 👎 2 ⊘ Rate This

But I thought we were supposed to believe Bill when he denies having ever gotten more than one dox wrong?

And just because you are now "friends" with the woman in OR, doesn't mean that you didn't get the dox wrong, you platyhelminthic idiot.

If you mean "Tapeworm," SAY "Tapeworm," dummy!

WMS-DB
@WmsDb

Follow

Apparently Nancy thinks denying is the same as disproving. Like her hubby "denying" he's been unfaithful.

6:12 PM - 4 Oct 2014

Reply

125

librarygruffon   October 4, 2014 at 6:33 pm

👍 5 👎 0 🔘 Rate This

And given that Bill thinks that tweet suggesting my husband hasn't kept his marriage vows is somehow going to upset me, it is obvious that he thinks/knows that either he or/and Gail haven't been too good about keeping their's.

Reply

It's obvious you're a numbskull, Nanc.

 Techno Jinxx   October 4, 2014 at 6:49 pm

👍 3 👎 0 🔘 Rate This

His dox of Kimberly isn't just doubtful, it's plain out wrong, I know both her and Rain.
They are a study in opposites except for both being female.
Of course Shakey will never admit this, just like he'll never admit it's possible that someone may know Heather, the girl that passed and that she filed a domestic abuse complaint against Heather, without actually being Heather himself.

wah wah wah,blah blah blah, more assumptions and more lies, that's all Shakey's got.

Sure you do, Techno Boy.

librarygruffon   October 4, 2014 at 6:57 pm

👍 4 👎 0 🔘 Rate This

So true. It's amazing that the only person who could know about a restraining order is the person who went to court for it. And that that person is the only one who could know that the object of the restraining order had died. I mean obviously her family and other friends would never know about it!/sarc

Get a room, you two!

librarygryffon   **October 4, 2014 at 7:15 pm**

👍 3 👎 0 🔄 Rate This

Oh, and Bill, since he's obviously reading this: I have never mentioned his spouse, except in things such as saying I hope she is doing well when health issues have been brought up. He is the fucking asshole who brings in spouses, parents, children, friends, etc. So, I'm sorry I ever said nice things to him about his wife. He obviously enjoys people saying bad things about her, because either he agrees with them, or at least it gives him one more thing to complain about; if nothing else, he lives to complain. I'm sure that if he were to end up in heaven (and that ain't happening the way he are behaving right now) I'm sure he'd bitch about his wings being the wrong color, and how he can't stand that type of music, and why isn't there any gay porn?

Reply   ## Right. I bring in the families.

 EPWJ   **October 4, 2014 at 8:08 pm**

👍 4 👎 1 🔄 Rate This

same with my kids

What about your kids? They find out Daddy's not "quite right in the head?"

 Neal N. Bob   **October 4, 2014 at 6:30 pm**

👍 4 👎 1 🔄 Rate This

It seems to me that William is forever decrying the failure of the constabulary to respond to his pleas, yet always assumes that the next time will be different.

There is a clinical definition for that, you know.

Reply   ## Kneeling Bob is RIGHT!

 EPWJ   **October 4, 2014 at 6:46 pm**

👍 2 👎 3 🔄 Rate This

dumb? beyond stuuuplid

Army Vet   October 4, 2014 at 6:48 pm

👍 5 👎 1 ⊘ Rate This

Good God, doesn't he ever get tired of being the failure? Seriously when has he ever got
anything right? Court cases? Bragged and yelled about the "smoking gun" that would win him in
case how many times? Worked? 0. Fail after fail after fail. And he never learns.

Reply   **Don't you ever get tired of printing the same crap over
                 and over and over and over again?**

🔲 *EPWJ*   October 4, 2014 at 7:24 pm

👍 4 👎 3 ⊘ Rate This

Email sent describing Bills recent attempts to file false charges against people and his ties to
known felons. Sent screen shots of his posting pictures of young girls without permission on his
websites   **Who said the charges were false? Have they been
Reply   adjudicated yet? Is it against the law to know a felon?
                 What screen shots of young girls?**

🔲 *EPWJ*   October 4, 2014 at 7:25 pm
                              **Ah. To help prove my case.
👍 2 👎 3 ⊘ Rate This   Thank you, Eric.**

To the Racine Sheriff's office

Reply

128

Kyle Kiernan   October 4, 2014 at 7:38 pm

👍 3 👎 0 ⊙ Rate This

It's a little sad making to be one of his complete dox fails. If he doesn't have a clue who you really are he mostly ignores you out of fear he'll demonstrate his ass dumbness. But if he thinks he's got a pretty good bead on your ID he'll poke and respond.

Why is this a drag? I don't troll him cuz I'm looking for enlightenment or edification but because I like the verbal strike and riposte. I'm here for the insult and the outrage and sometimes I get to trigger the Feltdown.

PS: This topic got chopped from HW but I still think its a valid question as to whether or not he gave his wifey cancer. Munchausen' by Proxy is known and diagnosable syndrome and he sure do love the attention.   **Your denying who you are doesn't make me wrong,**
                                  Kyle. And you are utter slime for suggesting I gave my
Reply   **wife cancer. Whose mind WORKS like that?**

> *librarygruffon*   October 4, 2014 at 7:41 pm
>
> 👍 3 👎 1 ⊙ Rate This
>
> I can't talk to that, but he does love anything that makes him look the victim. He seems to always discuss his wife's health issues as minor things unless he thinks he can use them to show what off what a good husband he is, or to garner sympathy for himself.
>
>   **You can talk to that, Dim Girl. When did I ever say my**
> Reply   **wife's cancer was a "minor issue"?**
>
> > *Howard D. Earl (@embryriddlealum)*   October 4, 2014 at 8:03 pm
> >
> > 👍 4 👎 0 ⊙ Rate This
> >
> > Or to explain her Irish Sunglasses.
> >   **Tee hee hee! Because I'm a WIFE beater, right Chrissy?**
> >   **Did you know Stacy Thomas has sisters living in Racine?**

Howard D. Earl (@embryriddlealum)　　　　October 4, 2014 at 8:02 pm

👍 5 👎 1 ⊘ Rate This

Nope, Shakey. I'm not Chris H.

I'm not from Wisconsin.

NOTHING will happen to me.

NOTHING.

Everyone point and laugh at Inspector Shake and Flake.

Reply

Sure are crying a lot for someone with nothing to worry about, Chrissy!

 Neal N. Bob　　　　October 4, 2014 at 8:08 pm

👍 5 👎 0 ⊘ Rate This

Did you get your three million from Hoge and Krendler, William? Did you keep your "fair use" postings up? How about the infringing books, dear boy? Are they still on the market?

You do see why one would dispute your legal acumen, wouldn't you?

Reply

Did I do the suing? Did Hoge win a thing? I think I did fairly well, thank you.

 EPWJ　　　　October 4, 2014 at 8:09 pm

👍 5 👎 0 ⊘ Rate This

forgot the reviews – were they removed?

Reply

Do even YOU know what you're talking about?

　　Grace　　　　October 4, 2014 at 9:13 pm

One of these days, Gracey McHate is gonna 'SPLODE!

👍 3 👎 0 ⊘ Rate This

And, remember when @ mentions on Twitter were NOT direct contact? Heh.

Good times. Good times.

Yet, the bloated bastard for some reason refuses to @ mention Hoge.

Howard D. Earl (@embryriddlealum)   **October 4, 2014 at 8:18 pm**

👍 5 👎 1 ⭐ Rate This

"And the fact that after all of this time no one has even TRIED to explain it..."

That drives you bugshit, Shakey.

I like that. I like that a lot.

Reply   **Well, no Chris. It pretty much proves there IS no explanation for it.**

 Howard D. Earl (@embryriddlealum)   **October 4, 2014 at 8:25 pm**

👍 5 👎 1 ⭐ Rate This

"It's in the hands of Law Enforcement. We'll see what THEY come up with."

I can tell you right now. Look in the mirror, Shakey.

See that big, fat fucking ZERO? That's what they will come up with.

Everyone limber up their LULZ muscle for some fun.

Because I have.....   **Jesus. The whining. If you whine that much in jail, they're gonna find a special use for you, Chris.**

Reply

 librarygryffon   **October 4, 2014 at 8:46 pm**

👍 3 👎 0 ⭐ Rate This

Good lord, his twitter feed looks like the Flow Chart with only yes options he made to prove that Causey was Howard. But since he already KNEW that Howard is Chris, he must have figured that somehow Chris lived in both Racine by himself, and in AZ with a wife and child.

And actually, a *lot* of us are hoping that death bed comes soon. So I guess he needs to report every single person who reads and posts here to Elkridge PD as sending death threats too.   **It gratifies me that my stalkers have such total recall of my every post!**

I'd love to here the tape of *that* 911 call. LOL

Grace — October 4, 2014 at 9:17 pm

2 0 Rate This

I laughed hard at that tweet... Death Threat ELEVENTY!!1!!1!1!

Hoping an evil spawn of Satan soon meets his demise does NOT a death threat make.

When do the dudes with the XXXXX white jacket show up? He keeps this nonsense up with local law enforcement much longer... I definitely see a 5150 in his near future.

Someone did something bad to you once, right? And you're taking it out on me.

librarygryffon — October 4, 2014 at 9:59 pm

2 0 Rate This

Your fingers to God's eyes......   **...or nose, whichever.**

And, you get the point.

12 FIRST THEY SAY I DO, AND THEN I DON'T

Depending on what day it is, perhaps even on what TIME of day it is, I either do have Parkinson's disease, do NOT have Parkinson's disease, am wildly crazed with Parkinson's dementia, type too fast to have Parkinson's disease, or have been exaggerating my fake symptoms to get sympathy.

Howard Hanger-Earl (@embryriddlealum)
on 17 May, 2014 at 16:23 said:

👍 17 👎 0 ⊘ Rate This
I hope his phony Parkinson's disease was acting up and he had to use his voice software.

It's like being stalked by the McDonald's drive through speaker.

Neeland Bob (@embryriddlealum)
on 14 April, 2014 at 19:52 said:

👍 7 👎 0 ⊘ Rate This
Profundity has never been his strong suit. He is easily confused. Fake Parkinson's and all.

Originally posted on The Thinking Man's Zombie:

I had thought before now that only John Hoge possessed the power to manipulate men's minds. Then I thought that perhaps I had a small degree of talent at dragging certain people to my blog to be offended. This may be true; surely more scientific study is required. Does anyone know how to contact Drs. Stantz, Venkman & Krendler?

Anyway, that's what I thought until earlier today when I received what was an unmistakable psychic message:

Dear Paul,

Gail and Dr. Grill have both threatened to take my computer away if I continue blogging and tweeting. Would you please replace all my fucked-up comments with this message, and ban me because I have dementia, a full pair of Depends, and no impulse control whatsoever?

Thanks

A clear request for a voluntary ban. I was powerless to resist!

If I had been faking my Parkinson's, I would say, "Hey, that's really devotion to a bit, having two divots dug out of his head just to fool people he doesn't know or care about that he has a disease that they don't believe he has and he could not care one way or the other what these mouth-breathing cretins think about his condition.

I talk about my Parkinson's because it is a large part of my life. It is why I am retired and have been since 2011. It affects every single aspect of my life, my sleeping, my ability to write, my thinking, what I eat, what I drink, how I take care of my daily needs, all of that. Let's face it. It's a brain thing.

I have mentioned that I am noticing some early signs of Parkinson's dementia. Naturally, to my trolls, that means something that it doesn't really mean, nor will it ever mean.

But, we're talking about trolls here. Their job is to crap on everything I say or do.

My Deep Brain Stimulation surgery, for instance. The trolls say it's no big deal because people have DBS every day. (Not the SAME person, you know, but PEOPLE in the generic use of the word.)

And that is true. But only under conditions approved by the Food and Drug Administration.

There are 15 people in the United States who have had this operation in the early stages of PD.

And some people think it was a pretty big deal.

Events honor early patients of novel Parkinson's study

by Leslie Hill | Posted on Thursday, Aug. 23, 2012 — 8:24 AM

From left, Wayne Holt, Dale Nevels, Duane Cook and Bill Schmalfeldt are among the group of patients who volunteered for Vanderbilt's study into using deep brain stimulation (DBS) to treat late-stage Parkinson's disease.

Pioneers of Parkinson's disease research are gathering at Vanderbilt University Medical Center today to celebrate the end of a study that was an important first step in the quest to find a way to slow the progression of the degenerative movement disorder.

In 1997, the FDA approved a treatment for late-stage Parkinson's called deep brain stimulation (DBS). The therapy, manufactured by Medtronic, involves a thin wire implanted deep in the brain running to a small pulse generator implanted under the collarbone that emits an electrical current.

While DBS is an accepted therapy for patients not helped by medication, there is no treatment proven to slow the progression of Parkinson's.

"There is the possibility that if deep brain stimulation is applied early, it can slow down the disease," said David Charles, M.D., professor and vice-chair of Neurology and principal investigator of the study.

But before this theory could be tested, there needed to be an initial safety and tolerability study to ensure that giving early DBS would not cause unforeseen problems.

Beginning in 2006, 35 research subjects were recruited, given a thorough explanation of the risks, and randomized to receive DBS or be part of a standard of care control group.

The phase 1 clinical trial was the first and only of its kind in the world to test DBS in such an early stage of Parkinson's disease.

"There were a lot of questions surrounding this study. Patients can expect five to seven good years on medication alone, so is it ethical to expose them to the risk associated with surgery when the group had only been on medicine an average of two years? One patient did have a mild stroke following surgery and is cognitively impaired. That's where the rubber meets the road about people stepping up because the risks are real," Charles said.

"Then there were questions about whether patients, since they had decided they wanted the surgery, would drop out if they were randomized to medicine. But only one patient dropped out."

Charles said these 35 volunteers are a special group.

"I've gotten to know these people. They are a very spiritual group, and helping others was the resounding sentiment and at the core of why many wanted to join the study."

For Janet Frazer, a first-grade teacher who retired to the mountains in Fairfield Glade, Tenn., it's exciting to be in the first group of research subjects that could potentially lead to a cure.

"After reading so much about Parkinson's, I decided I wanted to be involved in research. It's so important to solving many of our medical problems. I feel very blessed in my life — I could easily have been diagnosed with something worse — and the least I could do was give back," Frazer said.

Frazer was randomized to the standard of care group, which took the medications typically given to Parkinson's patients.

Duane Cook, a lawyer from Georgetown, Ky., said the participants receiving standard of care like Frazer made the biggest sacrifice.

"I was interested in anything that would slow the progression," he said. "I knew there was a risk in surgery, but that paled in comparison to the risk of early dementia. It would have been hard not to have the surgery. Those people are the real heroes."

Cook, who opened his own law firm at 59 and is an avid golfer, said his disease has not progressed.

"I work at the keyboard every day and golf all the time. Most people wouldn't look at me and say I've got Parkinson's."

In addition to agreeing to the risky surgery, study participants also committed to five weeklong stays at VUMC's Clinical Research Center over a two-year period.

For Dale Nevels, a manufacturer's representative in Memphis who received DBS, those visits were a glimpse of life without any treatment options.

"I'd call it hell week. The first day they stopped all [Parkinson's] medications and turned off the neurostimulators. It took a few days to float to the bottom of the ocean, and they would do tests," he said.

"Then I was plugged back in and floated back to the top. It was so psychologically and physically demanding. And I would always say, 'thank goodness I have had the surgery.'"
Many of the participants keep in touch and even play golf regularly.

At the gathering today, they will learn the results of the study, which will be formally published in the winter, and hear presentations from French scientist Alim-Louis Benabid, who was the first to use DBS to treat movement disorders in 1987, and Caryl Sortwell, Ph.D., professor in the Division of Translational Science and Molecular Medicine at Michigan State University, who is conducting basic science research that may explain how early stimulation could be neuro-protective.

"It was a tough decision to join the study, and these volunteers gave a huge amount of time, so we feel an obligation to give back to them and share what we learned from them," Charles said.

On Aug. 25, VUMC is leading a national consortium of more than 20 neurologists and neurosurgeons from academic medical centers around the country to discuss the next steps of researching DBS for early-stage Parkinson's disease.

While the results are still pending on the safety and tolerability of the approach, planning has begun for the next stage of the study — a large, multi-national, multi-center trial.

"This is how new therapies come about — partnerships between universities, industry and patient volunteers," Charles said. "The patients in this study deserve all the credit. They are truly heroes because they stepped up to accept potentially devastating consequences in hopes of helping others with Parkinson's disease in the future."

Ah. But not everyone agrees.

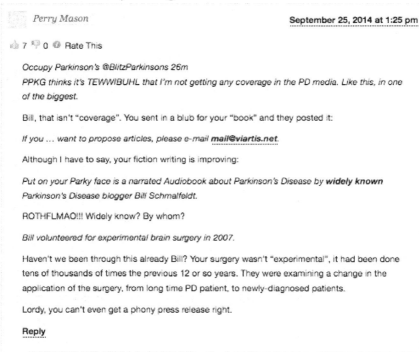

Perry Mason   September 25, 2014 at 1:25 pm

👍 7 👎 0 ⊘ Rate This

Occupy Parkinson's @BlitzParkinsons 26m
PPKG thinks it's TEWWIBUHL that I'm not getting any coverage in the PD media. Like this, in one of the biggest.

Bill, that isn't "coverage". You sent in a blub for your "book" and they posted it:

If you ... want to propose articles, please e-mail **mail@viartis.net**.

Although I have to say, your fiction writing is improving:

Put on your Parky face is a narrated Audiobook about Parkinson's Disease by **widely known** *Parkinson's Disease blogger Bill Schmalfeldt.*

ROTHFLMAO!!! Widely know? By whom?

Bill volunteered for experimental brain surgery in 2007.

Haven't we been through this already Bill? Your surgery wasn't "experimental", it had been done tens of thousands of times the previous 12 or so years. They were examining a change in the application of the surgery, from long time PD patient, to newly-diagnosed patients.

Lordy, you can't even get a phony press release right.

Reply

 *Kyle Kiernan*   September 26, 2014 at 9:32 am

👍 6 👎 0 ⊘ Rate This

guy gets a couple coat hangers stuck in his noggin and starts thinkin he's the second coming instead of just a failed retroactive abortion

 *Paul Krendler*   **September 25, 2014 at 4:07 pm**

👍 10 👎 0 ⊙ Rate This

I'm sorry, but the 30 second DOOM CLOCK has expired, and there is no allowance in Society of Professional Cyberstalking Journalists Code of Ethics for extending the arbitrary DOOM CLOCK deadline for an excess of accomplishments.

Please pick up your sewing machine and mouthwash beside the exit to your right. Thank you for playing.

NEXT!

Reply

> *Howard D. Earl (@embryriddlealum)*   **September 25, 2014 at 4:38 pm**
>
> 👍 3 👎 0 ⊙ Rate This
>
> Someone is going to have Pennywise the clown with the voice of a McDonald's drive-thru speaker harassing them this evening?
>
> Just kill yourself, Bill. Gail will thank you.
>
> Take the CURE, Bill.
>
> .45 ACP should be enough.

> *Gus Bailey*   **September 26, 2014 at 9:29 am**
>
> 👍 4 👎 0 ⊙ Rate This
>
> Skull's too thick. .45 ACP has lots of energy, but it's all mass. For something that pig-headed a .308 has much more penetrating power.

 Perry Mason   **September 25, 2014 at 3:55 pm**

👍 9 👎 0 ⊙ Rate This

Occupy Parkinson's @BlitzParkinsons · 20s
Quick. Shitweasels. Name one thing you've done in your lives that gives you pride.

I had some hemorrhoids removed. They tell me it was "experimental".

Reply

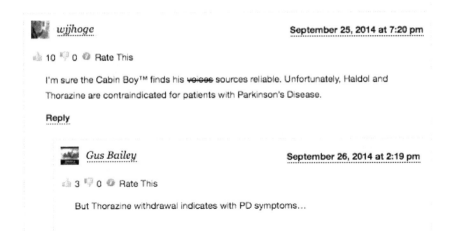

You see? It's important that I not be allowed to have any sort of accomplishment of which to be proud. This torrent came when I blogged that the clinical trial I was part of had been given FDA approval for a much larger, Phase III trial, involving hundreds of patients in America and Europe.

But it's important to the trolls to shit on each and every accomplishment I've had, to downplay or deny it, because a GOOD and DECENT me that most people who actually KNOW me LIKE or LOVE?

That doesn't fit the Doctrine or the Canon. Such things must be considered apocryphal and never ever included into the official Dogma.

13 WHAT TO DO?

The answer is simple, really.

ENFORCE THE FREAKIN' LAW!!!

Here in Maryland, we already have laws against Internet Harassment on the book. But the police will not investigate complaints. And under Maryland's quaint "citizen report" system, one can waltz into a Court Commissioner's office, allege a crime has been committed, present scant evidence, swear that he or she is telling the truth, and charges are filed. This puts the State's Attorney in the position of the police investigator, and with as many violent crimes they have to worry about, they're just not going to bother with some guy with Parkinson's disease who has had quite enough with the death threats and doesn't want to wait until someone actually carries one out before the cops will do anything.

Oh, we have dandy laws in Maryland to protect teenagers from online bullying. Why is there no law protecting adults from the same?

Why don't the ISPs follow their own Terms of Service?

Why does Twitter suspend the complainer without touching the reason for the complaint?

The laws are in the books!

2010 Maryland Code
CRIMINAL LAW
TITLE 3 - OTHER CRIMES AGAINST THE PERSON
Subtitle 8 - Stalking and Harassment
Section 3-805 - Misuse of electronic mail.

§ 3-805. Misuse of electronic mail.

(a) "Electronic mail" defined.- In this section, "electronic mail" means the transmission of information or a communication by the use of a computer or other electronic means that is sent to a person identified by a unique address and that is received by the person.

(b) Prohibited.- A person may not use electronic mail with the intent to harass:

(1) one or more persons; or

(2) by sending lewd, lascivious, or obscene material.

(c) Construction of section.- It is not a violation of this section for any of the following persons to provide information, facilities, or technical assistance to another who is authorized by federal or State law to intercept or provide electronic mail or to conduct surveillance of electronic mail, if a court order directs the person to provide the information, facilities, or technical assistance:

(1) a provider of electronic mail;

(2) an officer, employee, agent, landlord, or custodian of a provider of electronic mail; or

(3) a person specified in a court order directing the provision of information, facilities, or technical assistance to another who is authorized by federal or State law to intercept or provide electronic mail or to conduct surveillance of electronic mail.

(d) Exception.- This section does not apply to a peaceable activity intended to express a political view or provide information to others.

(e) Penalty.- A person who violates this section is guilty of a misdemeanor and on conviction is subject to imprisonment not exceeding 1 year or a fine not exceeding $500 or both.

But instead of enforcing the laws as written, the overworked police department tells the victim to sue the bastard. Which is all well and good, if you have a few thousand bucks to drop on a lawyer. Even if you want to go the pro se route and represent yourself, there's a huge filing fee.

And who can pick up and travel from Maryland to Tennessee to sue someone for posting false, negative reviews on Amazon? Who can jump on a plane and fly to Wisconsin to sue some unwashed dirtbag for libel?

I can't tell you how many times I've heard a judge say, "I don't know anything about Twitter, but…"

Well, then LEARN! FIND OUT WHAT YOU'RE RULING ON! DON'T MAKE A RULING BASED ON IGNORANCE!

Knowledge of the Internet and its laws should be

required of everyone who puts on a judicial robe. This is 2014. This stuff has been around for awhile. I can't believe there are judges who still don't know how to send an e-mail or use a cell phone, let alone make rulings involving the use of technology they do not understand.

But such is how things are. I don't see things changing any time soon.

The laws are in the books.

I was raised to believe that your right to swing your arm ends at the tip of my nose. Your right to exert your freedom of expression ends when your expression causes me harm, or puts me in actual fear for my life, my family, my pets and my property.

Talking to the trolls, asking them to stop. You're wasting breath. You're using perfectly good pixels that could be used for something else. These people like what they're doing. The vast majority of the ones I find myself dealing with have no blogs of their own, their Twitter accounts are private, and there is no recourse to answer them.

When you do answer them, and if they can lie to a judge about how blocking you on Twitter is the same as disabling a portion of their Internet functionality, you get a peace order (restraining order) placed against you.

And when you're ill with a progressive neurological disorder that is made worse by stress, and your adversaries know this and intentionally inflict stress in the hopes of killing you without getting their hands dirty, there needs to be a basic level of protection in place.

We pay our taxes. We are citizens. We are owed the full protection of the law under our local laws, state laws, state constitutions, the US Code and the Constitution of the Unites States.

Your ability to defend your family from online monsters should not depend on your ability to pay for an attorney.

 Springtime 4 Pundit @PalatinePundit 4h
@LibraryGryffon Mr. Bill says, "OOOOOOOOOOOOOOOOOOOOH
NOOOOOOOOOOOOOOOOO!" @ParkyBillTweets
pic.twitter.com/dHcaTW3gKY

↩ Reply ⇄ Retweet ★ Favorite   Flag media

ABOUT THE AUTHOR

William M. Schmalfeldt, Sr. is everything his detractors say he is. You should not believe a word he says. He posts pictures of young girls on blogs, and he forces them to eat bits of brain for the entertainment of the New World Order and their Black Helicopters. He once dug up a dead baby, put it into a gaily wrapped Christmas Present box, handed it to the baby's father who screamed and fainted when he opened the box to see the loathsome package within. While he lay there on the floor, unconscious, Schmalfeldt tore the dead baby into small pieces and crammed it down the father's throat and the grieving mother stood there weeping. He has also written some books and audiobooks and stuff.

--EPWJ

OTHER WORK BY THIS AUTHOR

Put On Your Parky Face!: The Expanded Version [Unabridged] [Audible Audio Edition]
by Bill Schmalfeldt (Author), William M. Schmalfeldt (Narrator)
Be the first to review this item

Listen on your **Kindle Fire** or with the **free Audible app** on Apple, Android, and Windows devices.

Formats	Amazon Price	New from	Used from
Hardcover	—	$72.63	—
Audible Audio Edition, Unabridged	$17.46		

The Lord of Satire
Bill Schmalfeldt (Artist)   Format Audio CD
⭐ 1 customer rating · 1 customer review

Price: **$12.00**

In Stock.
Want it Friday, Oct. 10? Order within 12 hrs 16 mins and choose **One-Day Shipping** at checkout. Details
Sold by Amazon.com. Gift-wrap available.

	Amazon Price	New from	Used from
Audio CD, September 9, 2014	$12.00	$12.00	

CD-R Note: This product is manufactured on demand when ordered from Amazon.com. [Learn more]

Look inside ↓

Flip to back

See all 2 images

Baby's First Book of Socialist Propaganda Paperback – September 8, 2014
by William M Schmalfeldt Sr. (Author)
⭐ 2 customer ratings · 2 customer reviews

· See all 2 formats and editions

Kindle	Paperback
$0.00 kindleunlimited	$8.82
Subscribers read for free	3 New from $8.82
$5.00 to buy	

Imagine a post-apocalyptic America, fragmented beyond recognition. People will still, no doubt, have babies. And, if current trends hold (we're looking at YOU, Texas) the fragmented nation will want the children in their individual fragments to learn the history THEY want the kids to learn. In that spirit we present "Baby's First Book of Socialist Propaganda". Written by some future bureaucrat to instruct the conservative children in this conservative group of former states, you can laugh at what is already happening in conservative states as the textbooks are changed to reflect the Tea Party ideology of the ruling powers. Here's the original product description: There are no pretty pictures in this book. Pretty pictures are for soft minds. Do you want your children to be soft-minded? No. You do not. Soft minds are for liberals, and they are the weaklings we are fighting in the east. You want your children to be strong, liberty-loving, free-thinking patriots who will do as we say. You will begin reading chapters from this
· Read more

THANK YOU FOR READING THIS!

www.ingramcontent.com/pod-product-compliance
Lightning Source LLC
Chambersburg PA
CBHW071000050326
40689CB00014B/3434